Finding Myself

Discovering My Gender Identity

Karen Lyra

Title: "Finding Myself: Discovering My Gender Identity"

Published in 2021 & Updated in 2023

Cover: Sasha Freemind (www.unsplash.com)

Author: Karen Lyra.

Email: karenlyra69@gmail.com

Instagram: karenlyra_findingmyself

Thanks to Jennifer Swanson for her editing assistance.

To that little girl whose voice I didn't hear
when she was trying to show me the path
when everything was confused and dark
until the time came when I realized
she was not just a voice
but she was my inner self
struggling to find her place in this world.

We are born humans,

and as humans, we live,

trying to become the best version of ourselves,

trying to fulfill our dearest dreams.

Karen Lyra

Table of contents

Why Did I Write This Book?

I thought about writing this book several years ago. After the idea came to me I wondered why I had that thought, why had I started to feel that I should open my soul to express myself and get deeply in contact with that "part of me" I have suppressed for most of my life. I was afraid to answer my question because I was sure it was going to be like opening a door and entering a path for which the only way out was to keep on moving forward until it ended where I would find my true self standing there. Once I stepped onto that path there would be no turning back and that scared me because I could sense the impact it would have on me and in my life. Having many fears and worries in my heart, I avoided giving more of my thoughts to the idea of the book, but it kept coming back as time passed by until it became impossible to ignore it anymore and it was time to do something about it.

"Finding myself" is an inner journey I decided to start some years ago about the decisions I made in my life to help me understand who I am. Writing this book has become a crucial part of that journey and a definitive milestone in my life.

I realized I was transgender a few years ago and became aware that I have lived all my life not suppressing a part of me, as I once thought, but suppressing my true self. Given the stage of life I am going through, with its circumstances, challenges, and blessings, maybe it is going to take more time to achieve my desired changes, but it is not fair to keep my true self in the dark any longer. I haven't come out in real life yet and it may be a while before I take that step. I want to put my words out there to share all that I have been through since the very first moment of my life that I wanted to be a girl. By writing this book I am giving myself the chance to ease the turmoil in my head and as a way of reaching other souls that might be in a similar situation with their gender identity, and possibly let these lines be part of what they need to read to move forward in the path of their own journey.

Finding Myself

"Finding Myself" was the original title of my blog on Tumblr in 2019 where I began to share pictures and thoughts about my feelings towards my gender identity. I decided to start that blog after several years of being on Facebook and Instagram where I began my first virtual activity in social networks with the transgender community. It was very surprising for me how the virtual interaction with men and women from all around the world helped me understand the transgender community and myself. It was a wonderful discovery.

I was very active on social networks, posting, chatting, and subscribing to some sites and groups to research and learn as much as I could. I didn't know I could make friends like in the real world, although I haven't met them personally, the level of interaction I achieved with them and what we shared about our lives gave us a bond we will never forget.

From time to time I found myself reaching a point where questioning my gender identity and how I was feeling by not being able to express the real me in the real world was causing too much stress. In those moments I decided to stay offline for long periods that included deleting my profiles on those social networks. Then a friend I met on Facebook wrote me an email sharing a link to a post on Tumblr where a picture of me was posted in a blog of crossdressers. It was the first time I realized that whatever is shared on the Internet can be used by anybody else in any way they want, and from the moment we publish a picture of us we are losing control of where that picture may end up. I didn't know about Tumblr until that moment and realized what I have shared on other social networks and sites could be flying around corners of the Internet I had no idea existed even if I had deleted my content and profiles. Even though I never posted any type of nude or explicit pictures, I found one of my photos being used in promotion of an adult sex site. That was not what I wanted to happen with my content. I contacted those persons that were using my pictures and I was successful in getting them off those sites, but only for a while. It happened with another picture on another site, and I understood it was not going to be something I could stop. That was when I thought I needed to do something else. If someone was using my old deleted pictures in their blogs on Tumblr without my permission, then I should open a blog of my own.

I named the blog "Finding Myself" and started sharing my pictures dressed as a woman while learning the mechanics on Tumblr. I made a first attempt, but my blog ended more like a photo album as it happened before on other social networks. I wanted to do something different to express myself through the blog, besides sharing my pictures. I wanted to share something else and thought it could be better if I added content and context to my posts as a way to give insights into who I am, and what I have been through as a person with gender identity issues from as young as I can remember and trying to discover myself, my inner self as a woman, beyond the female figure, beyond the dresses, makeup, and high heels.

It was March of 2020, just before the Covid-19 pandemic forced quarantines where I live when I reopened my blog and began sharing my story while posting photos. I have been able to meet very interesting people and make wonderful friendships beyond the borders of my country. I didn't think I could end up feeling love and feeling loved by people that I hadn't had the chance to meet in person. Writing, sharing, answering questions, getting feedback, comments, etc. made me get deeper into my true identity and encouraged me to continue. I found there were some people like me for whom what I shared was useful for their journey into their gender identity research. I have found the whole experience in Tumblr to be rewarding in many ways and I thought I could venture into the project of writing this book to get deeper into what I have already shared and make it available to others.

Later in this book, I will explain how I realized I was transgender. It was a process that I believe may be like others, but deep inside I understand it is a personal quest. In my case, once I became aware of being transgender, many experiences I have had made sense to me and fell into place. Some made me happy and some made me sad. Even though that sensation of finally being conscious of who I am was something I was willing to pursue, it still took time to process the new awareness and accept it with an open heart. Getting to that awareness was like getting to the end of the quest and knowing how it was going to end but not wanting to reach that point for some unknown reason. With the new awareness and acceptance came the question of "What should I do now?" Preparing to answer that question is the beginning of a new journey, the beginning of another quest in which I may already know who I am but now the challenge is to keep moving forward on my way to find myself. How will it end? How long will it take? I don't know but it feels good and right to take steps in that direction.

About Me

I am Karen Lyra, a woman, although I was born with a male body and so my gender was assigned male at birth. I was given a boy's name and was the second child of a loving married couple that believed their love would last forever but that didn't happen. I am a woman that has not come out to the real world yet. I am married, I have children, I have a job, and I have virtues and faults as everybody does. None of my family and friends know about the story I feel I need to share, the identity I feel I need to express. The names of people and places I am going to mention on these pages have been changed on purpose because I value the privacy of the people in my life and the people I have met during my experiences as a transgender person. All the stories you will find here are not fiction, are not coming out of my imagination. All the events were key parts of my life that made up who I am today. I am not an expert on anything, not even an expert on my own life, but have come to an understanding about myself as a different person than who I thought I was and I feel the need to share my story.

I am grateful for the life I have lived, no matter the difficulties I was or am still going through. I embrace my blessings as well as my curses and try my best to learn from every experience. I had the chance to travel around the world for much of my life, to places I dreamed of and others I never imagined I would visit. I have practiced some religions but never feel at ease and I ended up practicing only love and finally found peace. I made promises to myself and others and tried hard to keep them but ended up breaking more than I would have liked to. I have lived a lucky life to witness many of my dreams coming true and to accept that some others may not happen or may take a bit longer. One of them is to be able to live the life of the woman I have always felt I am.

I love writing, I love music, I love the outdoors, I love nature, I love women, I love men. I love butterflies for their colorful wings, but I love more the caterpillars for their potential to transform themselves and fly away.

I believe in love regardless of gender and also believe that all of us, no matter from which walk of life we come, can generate a positive impact in our society, to generate hope that we all can do something for others and for ourselves to make this world a better and loving place where gender expressions are not a barrier to deal with, but a way to unify ourselves.

Part 1

Every story has a beginning. Thinking of writing about the very first moment when the idea that I wanted to be a girl came to me, I tried to understand what was possibly part of what happened to me before I can remember that may have conditioned my personality and the perception of myself I grew up with. If I was born a boy, why did I want to be a girl?

My parents already had a daughter, Nicole, who is two years older than me. After having a daughter my parents wanted to have a son and, when I was born, they were very happy to have completed the family the way they wanted. They named me Eric. My parents had many relatives and some of them were also having children at that time, so I ended up having many cousins although most of them were girls, especially the ones that were closer to my family.

I have some memories of when I was four years old, very vague, and not so clear, but I can remember. I have a pretty good memory and it is easy for me to go back to moments of my past when they have been emotionally powerful.

At four years old I started going to school and I remember crying a lot the first day when my mother and my father were leaving me there. I saw them leaving and felt terrible. I was too young to remember the thoughts I had back then, but the experience and my emotions are clear. As I was crying, I was taken to the classroom by a teacher, a lovely young woman named Miss Mary. She tried to comfort me and make me feel calm and stop crying. Miss Mary took me to a table where there was a girl in tears too. She and I were the only children crying at that moment and the others were staring at us. We had a label with our names on our aprons and Miss Mary introduced us and gave us a piece of paper with some crayons for us to draw and provide a distraction. The name of the girl was Lili and after a little while we were drawing quietly and became friends. We sat together for that first whole year at school and, as days and months passed, we made other friends too. However, I spent more time with Lili and other girls than with boys at school.

I don't remember being a child that caused trouble at home or school. I was more of the type that stayed quiet and obeyed without challenging my parents or other adults or children. Maybe that behavior triggered my dad's male chauvinist personality against me because he was a tall and strong man projecting the image of an alpha male while I was not projecting the image of the strong and brave son he wanted. He shouted at me a lot and hit me when my reaction was to cry if I felt bad about something or fell to the floor while playing. He yelled, "You are a boy, not a girl! Boys don't cry! You are strong! You are my son!". That was during the late '70s. He was very much like many of the stereotypical men and fathers of that time that I knew. When I was trying not to cry, I was deeply scared of being hit by him. He was very dominant and I remember the reaction of my mother at his behavior with me caused fights between them. Of course, there

12

must have been other factors causing them to fight but that was one, I am sure. When my father was not around, my mother comforted me and was always a very loving and caring woman. She didn't agree with how my father was treating me, though she never said directly to me that my father was doing something wrong. My father was traveling because of his job as an engineer, and I was spending most of my time playing with my sister Nicole and the female cousins that visited us from time to time. My mother tried to find a company for me with other boys. I was taken to visit some school classmates that were boys and made good friends with them.

During that first year at school, it happened that Lili asked me to stay in the classroom while most of the other children went out for recess. She was painting her nails using a red pencil and I was looking at her doing that and didn't go out to play. I stayed with her, and she asked me if I would let her paint my nails too. She showed me her nails while smiling at me. The color was not very noticeable, but she was so happy. She took my hand and put it over the table asking me to spread my fingers and then she took the red pencil and started coloring my nails the same as she did with hers. I remember how I felt when she was doing it. I liked the sensation of having my nails done by her and didn't feel ashamed or nervous. I didn't try to clean my nails either and wanted to happily show my mother what Lili had done to my nails. When I was back at home my mother noticed the traces of color on my nails and asked me about it and I told her. I don't remember any relevant reaction from my mother except that she only asked me to wash my hands and made no comment about it. It is strange when I think of it now because I do remember getting used to having Lili doing my nails many times at school that year but not getting any comments from my mother or anybody at school about it.

Some months after I turned five years old, my parents divorced. My father left my mother, Nicole, and me. He had another woman with whom he had another child, a boy. The separation hurt us all. My father disappeared for several years and during that time my mother, Nicole, and I moved to live with my mother's parents because she hadn't a job and needed financial help. I can remember seeing Nicole crying for my father. My mother cried a lot too. I cried because of seeing my mother and my sister very sad but I don't remember crying because my father was not with us anymore. Maybe it had to do with the fact that I felt safer once he was not at home because I was not going to be scolded or hit by him.

Until the moment my parents divorced, I had never tried on girls' clothes or had any thoughts about wanting to dress as a girl. My behavior was very normal for a child my age, but I didn't feel attracted to games that involved violence or fights, even if it was just pretending. Anyway, I was like another boy playing with the boys whenever I had the chance, but I also felt very comfortable playing with girls whenever those games had to do with playing "family" or being "father", "mother", "son" or "daughter". The other boys that were with me didn't like playing those games with girls and sometimes they said they didn't want to play with me because I liked playing with girls too much. I didn't feel bad or like something was wrong and I kept playing with boys or girls depending on the situation. I was very adaptable. I was a sort of submissive child that accepted playing games or doing things that others were asking me if I felt could be something I could enjoy. I could pretend to be Batman fighting The Joker sometimes, and I could

13

pretend to be the son of a beautiful queen of a faraway kingdom and let her dress and take care of me. I could play football with the boys, or I could jump rope with girls, being the only boy playing with them.

Thinking as I write about this part of my life, I understand I was never the child leading the games but the one following if it was something I really liked. At least at that young age. When my friends wanted to play as soldiers at war, I didn't want to, but I ended up playing with them to avoid being left alone. When my sister asked me to play with her Barbie dolls, I refused most of the time because I found that boring. However, I accepted playing with her dolls sometimes as she also accepted playing astronauts with me. I could adjust depending on who I was with, but I didn't have the concept that some games or toys were for girls or boys, or that pink was for girls and blue for boys. I was confused when hearing adults and children talking about "this is for girls" and "that is for boys" and nobody seemed to be able to explain that to me when I asked. Not even my mother. For me, I liked and disliked some stories of superheroes the same as I liked or disliked some stories of princesses. I was a fan of Luke Skywalker and Star Wars as much as I was a fan of Princess Aurora of The Sleeping Beauty tale.

That was the way I was at five years old and during that year of my life was when I wore girls' clothes for the first time. I remember the moment very well and I have thought deeply about that experience to find out why I did it, why I wanted to wear girl clothes at that young age, and how the event impacted me.

At school, boys were dressing differently from girls. We both were using aprons, but boys wore shirts and pants and girls wore blouses and skirts. Boys had short hair and girls had long hair in ponytails.

That second year at school Lili was in my classroom again. We sat together sharing the table as we did the previous year. She did not ask me to paint my nails again but one day she asked me to use her hairband. My hair was not short but not long. With my father at home I always had my hair cut very short as I can recall from the family pictures of that time but since he had left us my mother was not taking me to have my hair cut for quite a while and my hair was a bit longer than usual for boys of my age and it was going to grow longer. Lili put her hairband on me and adjusted my hair. She said I looked good and said I should let my hair grow longer so I can wear a ponytail like her. That made me think for the first time why couldn't I have my hair like hers or like other girls with laces, ribbons, hair clips, and ponytails? They looked beautiful and I thought I could look beautiful too. From that moment I didn't want to have my hair cut anymore and that became a problem with my mother later. While I had Lili's hairband on, one of the boys entered the classroom and Lili took her hairband off me immediately. I didn't think something was wrong, but it seemed Lili didn't want others to notice. She said something like: "My father says boys don't wear hairbands, but you looked good with it." "You can come to my house so we can play dress up together". Maybe those were not the exact words she used but it was something like that. I don't remember what my answer was, but when my mother picked me up from school, I asked her if I could go to Lili's house to play with her. Lili's invitation must have happened several times because I kept on asking my mother to take me to Lili's house, but she never did. I suspect the reason was that my mother wanted me to play with boys and not with girls.

14

One day I was at home back from school and went to my bedroom to change clothes and stay home. My sister's bedroom was close to mine, sharing a short corridor that could let us get to each other's bedrooms easily, just a couple of steps away. I took off my school uniform when I heard her calling me. I stepped into her bedroom in underwear looking for her. She was not there, and I found the skirt and blouse of her school uniform on her bed. She had already changed her clothes and had gone somewhere else. I looked at her skirt and blouse and just felt I should try on her clothes. I put the skirt on and liked how it looked on me. I don't remember my thoughts at that young age, but I do remember I liked wearing that skirt very much. Then I heard someone coming and I ran to my bedroom to hide, still wearing the skirt. Thinking about that moment has been very interesting. Why did I run away? Why did I want to hide? Why didn't I want to be seen dressing in a skirt? These questions made me think there must have been something happening before that experience with the skirt that made me think I was doing something wrong.

Trying to dig into my earliest memories to write about this experience I found what could be an important clue. It was a previous experience at five years old but just a bit earlier. My sister Nicole was playing at home with Laura, one of our cousins who was seven years old. She was staying with us during summer vacations. My mother asked my sister to go somewhere out with her and asked me to stay with Laura and play with her until they return. My grandparents were at home too, so Laura and I stayed with them. I asked Laura what she wanted to play. She said we could play dress up, the game she was about to play with my sister. She asked me to bring several of my clothes and we were going to mix them with clothes of herself and of my sister that they had already mixed before and put them all inside a basket. She said we were going to pick one piece of clothing from the basket but with our eyes closed and we should wear whatever we picked. I thought this was going to be a fun game, so I accepted. Thinking about it now is funny because it was obvious there were more chances of me ending up wearing girl clothes than Laura wearing my boy clothes. As innocent as children of our age, we were just having fun with no second thoughts about anything. Laura and I had fun and laughed while trying on the clothes. I remember we both were enjoying playing together a lot. At a point, we stopped picking clothes with our eyes closed and just chose whatever we wanted the other to try. She ended up fully dressed as a boy and I ended up fully dressed as a girl. We were openly laughing at each other and having fun. I can't remember all the clothes I tried but I enjoyed the game. It was all so natural and fun for us. When we finished playing and we were putting our own clothes back, I was still wearing one of Laura's blouses when her father, my uncle Robert, appeared. I don't know if he was staying at home that day or not but there he was. I remember my uncle looked at me and very angrily told me that I was a sissy because boys don't wear girls' clothes. All the fun vanished, and I felt very bad.

Looking at that event now I can imagine the attitude of my uncle Robert towards me for wearing a blouse that caused me to feel guilty, that I was doing something very wrong. The words and attitudes of adults can leave deep impressions on a child, for good or for bad. We should be very careful because kids may grow up keeping those things we as adults push into their minds, into their subconscious, even if we're not aware of it. They can affect the way children develop. So, after thinking about all this, I guess I ran away and tried to hide when I wore my sister's school skirt that first time because I remembered how much fun it was to wear girl clothes but I was also afraid of having someone mad at me, calling me "sissy" because I was "doing something wrong that boys are not supposed to do".

Given all the time that has passed since then, and all the other experiences I have had, I understand that was one of the key events of my life that had to do with gender identity issues. I think of it as one of the main events but not the only one, for sure. Other experiences also contributed a lot. The undeniable truth is that I liked wearing girls' clothes very much from as early as I can remember, as a natural way of choosing things we like when we were kids.

Wearing my sister's school skirt that day was the beginning for me. I managed to hide her skirt and then left it back on her bed later when nobody looked. At lunch with my mother, sister, and my grandparents, I was there but my mind was somewhere else. I was daydreaming that I could wear my sister's school uniform and go to school as a girl and play with Lili and the other girls. As a child, I was not thinking of any consequences and was wondering if I should tell my mother what I wanted. As the side of me that wanted to dress as a girl had started to grow, the side of me that was feeling guilty for wanting to do something that was supposed to be wrong was growing too and the inner turmoil started. I didn't tell my mother what I wanted but started looking for an opportunity to try my sister's school uniform at home again.

Finding out at that very young age that something was different in the way I felt about my gender made me think something was wrong with me. As I was growing older, that thought caused several periods of deep confusion. I was not yet six years old, and I had to hide my feelings as I had been told wearing dresses was something boys were not supposed to do. I didn't say anything about what I felt but at home, the conversations of adults on that topic made me think that way. My parents didn't approve that behavior. At a family gathering, I heard my uncle Robert telling my mother about the time he found me wearing Laura's blouse. My mother insisted that must have been just a kid's game, but my uncle insisted something was wrong with me because it seemed to him, he said, that I liked that. After listening to him I felt sad and confused and decided I should hide my feelings. I was afraid of telling my mother about it and it grew from that day without telling anybody. I am sure a strong wish was coming alive inside me, a wish that turned into the dream that one day I was not going to be a boy anymore and I was going to become a happy girl so nobody was going to tell me I can't wear dresses.

My wish of dressing again as a girl after that first time wearing my sister's school skirt turned into a desire to do it more times until I wanted to try some of her other clothes. I was careful to not be seen when trying them. I tried her panties once and felt so good that I repeated that many times. I had started the habit of sneaking into my sister's drawers and wearing her panties, t-shirts, and skirts whenever I could, but I wanted to see myself completely as a girl, and wearing panties or single pieces of girl clothing was soon not enough. I wanted to dress fully as a girl. It's strange to write it this way because I was too young, but the feelings were so strong that I can clearly remember how I was not thinking about the consequences and the possibility of being caught by my mother or sister wearing my sister's clothes.

It was a Friday and after we got home from school, Nicole left her uniform, skirt, socks, shoes, blouse, and hairband on her bed and went out to spend the weekend at Laura's house. When I realized she had left, I ran to her bedroom and took all her clothes to mine. I closed the door and dressed completely in her school uniform, completely careless, without thinking that my mother was still at home and my grandparents too. When I finished dressing and adjusted the hairband on my head, I went out of my bedroom to get to Nicole's bedroom to look at myself in the large mirror she had there. The moment I saw myself as a girl for the first time in a mirror was an amazing experience and a scary one too. I had just looked at myself and was daydreaming of going to school dressed like that when I heard my mother calling me. My reaction was to hide. I had no time to take the clothes off and I ran out of Nicole's bedroom to hide inside a big old closet. I could hear my mother's voice calling my name and moving around trying to find me. I was too scared and stayed hidden inside the closet. I could hear my mother getting worried and asking my grandmother if she had seen me and both were looking for me. I didn't know what to do. I didn't think about taking off the clothes and running somewhere else naked. I was just a small child and was scared that my mother was going to find me dressed as a girl and all I wanted to do was to cry. Dressed as a girl, I started to cry and sat down on the floor of the big closet hiding my face between my legs. I found a pencil on the floor and took it. The next thing I did was to write "I want to be a girl" on a hidden spot of that door. Moments after that, I reacted and took the clothes off, left them all hidden in the closet, and I ran naked to the bathroom. My mother did not catch me. I managed to get out without being seen until I had my boy's clothes on again.

Since that experience, those written words on the back of that door that came out of me at that moment have remained as a core thought about myself; a thought which I have struggled with between denial and acceptance for many years.

When I have been asked when I started crossdressing or thought that I wanted to dress as a girl, the short answer could be "when I was five years old" but the phrase itself without background and context seems to me like minimizing such a relevant and key event in my life. For me, it was more important to know the "Why?" than the "When?". I know many other girls like me that started at that same early age, some others started later when they were teenagers or adults. However, in my opinion, the story behind is what matters the most. Each person is a whole world in itself, their experiences are unique even if they sound similar because the traces and marks those experiences leave in one's soul are completely different.

The Party Dress

A couple of years passed. I continued to dress in my sister's clothes from time to time trying to be very careful to not be caught. I was around eight years old, and Nicole was ten and spending time with her girl friends at home or out. I was her "little" brother and she didn't want to play much with me anymore, so I was spending time on my own playing with my toys by myself. Having no brothers or male cousins close to us, our house was almost daily frequented by girl cousins or Nicole's girl friends from school. My mother was always trying to get me some company inviting boys from school to play with me at home or taking me to their houses. The latter was happening most of the time on weekends. We were sort of a medium to low-class level family, economically speaking, and my mother was making big efforts trying to cover our needs. Having Nicole and me out of home from time to time, I now know, was helping her by keeping us busy and with a company while she was working hard. My mother had two part-time jobs as a secretary, and she was also into making clothes for Nicole and me. She was also making dresses for some relatives and Nicole's girl friends to get some extra money. She was completely devoted to us and my grandparents were helping her take care of us at home as needed but could not be with us all the time. Sometimes I saw my mother working on her sewing machine at night when I was going to sleep and when I woke up the next morning, she was still there in front of her sewing machine working on the clothes she had to finish to get paid. At that moment I was just a kid and couldn't understand her sacrifice and efforts.

I developed a very close relationship with my mother and tried to help her at home with whatever was needed even if I was too young. I was still thinking that one day I should tell her what I was feeling about my desire to dress as a girl, my wish to be a girl. I was close to telling her many times, but I was too scared of her reaction and ended up giving up. In the meantime, when I was staying at home on weekends and Nicole was sleeping over at some friend's house, I took advantage of being alone and when my mother was sleeping or working very late, I managed to wear my sister's clothes secretly and carefully. Every time I was dressing as a girl, I had thoughts about what could happen if my mother discovered my crossdressing habits. What would her reaction be if she found me dressed as a girl? Would she like me as a girl? Would she accept me as her daughter?

During those days there was one time I was finally wearing a dress in front of my mother and sister. It was not that they caught me dressed, it was something I was asked to do. As my mother was used to making dresses for my sister and some of her girl friends, she was asked to make a party dress for Patty, one of those girls, because her birthday was approaching. Patty's mother told my mother the dress was intended to be a surprise, so my mother was not going to be able to ask Patty to try the dress on her but was able to take her measurements one day. I was at home playing near where my mother was working on the dress, and she came to me with a white silky party dress on her arm and asked me: "May I ask you a favor? This is Patty's birthday party dress that I am about to finish. I asked Nicole to try it on so I can check my work, but you know Patty is thinner and a bit shorter than her like you are. Will you try on this dress for me for a couple of minutes so I can check to be sure everything is fine?" My mother's voice was very tender and how she asked me was not like pretending I had to do it because she was asking me to. "If you don't want to, I understand. Don't worry", she added. I was confused. I really wanted to try the dress in front of her. I had already dressed many times in my sister's clothes in secret and had those feelings that I enjoyed dressing as a girl mixed with those thoughts that what I was doing was wrong. "I promised I will not tell anybody if you do it", my mother said trying to convince me as I had stayed in silence. I guess her last statement eased my confusion a bit and was also a sort of confirmation for my young mind that dressing as a girl was something I should keep hidden from others. I didn't say a word and accepted nodding my head. I undressed and stayed only in underwear in front of my mother. She put the party dress on me carefully until it was ready. It was the first time I felt a zipper being closed on my back. My mom asked me to stand in front of a mirror and started to go down on her knees to check the dress asking me to turn around while she was taking notes, adding a pin here and there. I was deep in silence looking delighted at myself in the mirror wearing that wonderful party dress. My mom finished very fast and stood by my side asking me to raise my hands to see how the dress lifted and confirm its length just a bit above my knees was right. She asked me to walk some steps, turn around and walk back to her. I felt like I was her girl model and loved that feeling. "This is good. I will need to work on a couple of things, but it looks beautiful", she said. Right at that moment Nicole appeared. She looked at me and opened her eyes wide, completely amazed. She was about to say something, and my mother interrupted her: "He is helping me as Patty is almost his size, so don't laugh at him and you will not say anything about this to anybody. Ok?". My mother's warning to my sister didn't stop me from feeling embarrassed as my sister did laugh a bit and then left. I blushed. What my mother said was a reaffirmation to me that something was not "right" about what I was doing even if I was helping her. She helped me take the dress off and noticed I was feeling bad. She gave me a kiss and a hug saying how grateful she was because I helped her. She also said I should not worry about Nicole telling anybody. My mother assured me she was going to take care of that. I was not feeling bad just because of my sister's attitude. I was feeling more embarrassed because while I really liked wearing that beautiful dress, my mother's words made it seem what I was doing was wrong. I didn't want her to know how much I liked wearing the dress. Why something that was making me feel so right, that made me feel so happy had to be taken as something wrong that should be hidden from others? I couldn't understand.

A couple of days later we went together to Patty's birthday party. She was looking so pretty wearing the white silky party dress. She was having fun twirling, dancing, and showing everyone how much she liked her dress, and how happy she was. I heard everyone say how beautiful she was that day and make nice comments about how she looked in that dress. I stared at her and thought about the time I helped my mother by wearing that dress and how pretty and happy I felt too but sad about why I couldn't enjoy it the way she did. "Isn't she pretty in that dress?", my mother asked me when she saw me looking at Patty. "Thank you for helping me with it", she said and kissed me. I think that was a chance to talk to my mother about what I was feeling but I couldn't find a way to overcome my fears and open up to her. Whenever I saw my mother working on a new dress, I wished she would ask me to try it on and be her model again. Unfortunately, I was not that lucky and it didn't happen again.

I was a child that fantasized a lot about being a model when I had the chance to dress in women's clothes. When my mother asked me to model for her that silky white party dress, I was in heaven. When I was watching TV and there was a fashion show on it, I imagined myself dressed as a girl modeling in public, but I was too afraid to show myself as a girl and I was sure I would never go up on stage as a model, not even in male clothes, because I was too shy.

One day I was unexpectedly asked to take part in a fashion show. It was a close friend of my mother who asked me for a favor. I was not yet a teenager and she told me they needed a boy to complete a group of models that were going to be a family on the show. The boy that was originally going to take part was sick and they needed a replacement. I didn't want to do it, but my mother insisted. I accepted not feeling good about the idea.

Days later I was at the backstage. There were few adult male models, and I was the only boy, but I didn't care because I was walking side by side with many beautiful female models. It was incredible to see how they were preparing, makeup, dresses, shoes, and hair, and I was amazed at the chance to be so close to them.

Our time to show arrived. Opposite to what I was expecting, I felt great. Maybe it was because the model playing the role of my mother was so kind and held my hand almost all the time which made me feel comfortable. She was a beautiful woman with such grace and sympathy, an image of beauty that was catching everybody's eyes. I felt so lucky to be with her and could feel how happy she was there doing what she loved.

After the show, I was told I did it well and was asked to join other shows. I accepted without hesitating. I was not going to miss the chance to be around those beautiful models and perform together letting through my imagination believe I was one of them.

On the day of the last show, I was happy to go out on stage again but also was feeling a bit sick. My mother asked me to stay home but I wanted to go because that was going to be the last one and I didn't want to miss having the experience again.

I was at the backstage wearing the boy clothes I was going to model together with Albert, the male model that was playing the role of the father. We were waiting for Natalie, the girl that was playing the role of the daughter, and Andrea, the woman that was playing the role of the mother. Albert asked me to go and look for Natalie and Andrea as our time to perform was coming. I walked through a corridor I was already familiar with and arrived at the door of the women's dressing room. Just before I knocked, Natalie opened the door and came out. I told her Albert and I were waiting for her and Andrea, and she rushed out to meet Albert leaving the door open. I knocked anyway and heard Andrea asking me to come in. Getting into the women's

21

dressing room was a dream that came true. I had always wanted to be there! I walked in and found Andrea standing beside a chair in front of a big mirror surrounded by lights, a big vanity full of makeup articles, and beautiful clothes and shoes around. Andrea was looking so beautiful as always and I was staring at her and the wonderful place in silence forgetting I was supposed to ask her to join us. She was looking for something on the floor and asked me for help.

-        Can you help me find an earring that just fell around here, please sweetheart? – she asked with her soft voice and the lovely attitude she always had with me. I searched for her earring on the floor and was lucky to find it at once.

-        Here you are! – I said smiling and satisfied to be able to help Andrea so fast.

-        You are awesome! Thank you, sweetheart! – she said very happy and put on her missing earring and then sat down again to retouch her makeup.

I watched Andrea's reflection in the mirror as she was applying setting makeup powder on her cheeks, under her eyes, nose, and chin, and then reapplied red lipstick carefully. While she was looking at herself in the mirror, she saw my reflection too and our eyes met. I think she noticed how marveled I was by being there with her and looking at how she was applying her makeup. She may have wondered why a boy was staring at her that way.

-        Are you ok, sweetheart? – she asked looking at me directly and not through the reflection in the mirror.

-        Yes. I'm sorry. They are waiting for us. – I answered a bit ashamed realizing she had noticed I was like hypnotized looking at her.

-        We'll go in a minute, but, are you ok? You look pale. – she said.

-        I was feeling a bit sick this morning, but I didn't want to miss performing in the show. – I answered. Andrea smiled at me and then gave a worried look to my face.

-        You are not looking good. You should have rested if you were not feeling okay, sweetheart. We can't perform on stage if we are not looking healthy, happy, colorful, and pretty. But you are lucky because I can help you with that. Makeup can work magic on us! – she said and very enthusiastically took a small round case from the vanity, opened it, and slightly applied some makeup powder on my face with a sponge. Then she took a makeup brush and applied some blush on my cheeks. I was so happy about what was happening and couldn't believe Andrea was applying makeup on me. Finally, she touched my lips repeatedly and softly with her fingertip applying something that smelled like lipstick.

-        And that's better. We want you to look handsome and healthy, and not girlie. – she said smiling while looking at me and taking off my lips a bit of what she put on them.

22

I looked in the mirror and could see some difference in my face, but not much. Of course, she didn't make me look like a girl and I secretly felt disappointed about that, but it didn't erase the happiness of that moment.

Performing in that last fashion show was a very enjoyable experience, even though I didn't dress as a girl. When I was there, walking with Andrea taking me from my hand, and looking at the crowd cheering and clapping, I felt transported to a magical world in which I was a beautiful female model enjoying being me. Modeling with Andrea and all those women fed my childhood dream of becoming a fashion supermodel like them one day.

As a kid, I was very innocent and believed that when I was dressing as a girl, I could become one sooner or later. I used to think it was just going to be a matter of growing up and one day I was going to be a girl. I was way too innocent.

Although I had developed my crossdressing habits, there were times that I just didn't think about that and behaved as any other kid of my age at school or home. There were times that I forgot about crossdressing or about my wish of one day becoming a girl. It was not something in my mind all the time and I was involved in common everyday activities.

I started to feel attracted to sports. I liked football and played at school although I was not very good at it but found a way to enjoy playing and making friends that were looking for me to play with them. I believe children can be influenced greatly when they find something they can do to make others happy or make others sad or mad. Somehow a child's behavior can be conditioned, but depending on the personality of the child, the influence can have a strong impact causing him or her to behave in a given way, aligned with that influence or condition, or resist that completely. I was not the kind of child that was going to speak up. I was shy, I felt scared that I would be punished or hit. I didn't want to fight and so I developed an introverted personality.

We had those activities at school in which we had to go in front of the class and tell everybody what we wanted to become when we grew up and why. I could not do it. I was too nervous to stand up in front of everyone. The teacher didn't push me when she realized I didn't want to do what I was asked but sent a note to my mother. When we were at home, my mother read the note and asked me what had happened. I couldn't explain it well. She was worried about me. She was sure something was not right with me and was trying different ways to get me to open up to her, but I couldn't. She thought it all had to do with my father leaving us and maybe she was right in some way. A divorce causes a big impact on children. Not having a father or a mother for whatever reason affects a child. Seeing the parents starting to live separate lives has an impact that we cannot calculate and sometimes we underestimate. I am not a psychologist, nor do I pretend to be an expert in a similar field. I am just talking about my own experience and coming to conclusions based on what happened to me, what I felt, and what I remember. It's kind of a logical thing anyway. How much and in which way does the impact of divorce change the behavior or the mindset of the child? It is not just one factor, I believe. But if the absence of a father or a mother or both are not well managed, the child is more likely to suffer.

During that time, I was sent to my mother to spend time with some school classmates at their homes on weekends which deeply marked my life and forced me to become shier and more introverted.

My mother became a very good friend of the parents of a boy in my class named Henry. Henry was their only child and because they were a very rich family, he had everything he wanted in terms of toys, clothes, activities, etc. He lived in a huge house with a swimming pool and a big

24

backyard, and her parents had another house at the beach. He had everything he wanted except a sibling with whom he could enjoy all that. My mother agreed with his parents to send me with them on several weekends and for an entire week too when we were on vacation. In the beginning, I enjoyed going there and staying with Henry. Other boys were going to his house and every day was like having a group of at least six boys and we played many things. I got along with them very well and became friends with them all. Some of them also stayed overnight at Henry's house so we were three or four sleeping over until I was invited to stay one week with Henry and his grandmother at their beach house. His parents were traveling and asked my mother if I could stay with Henry. I was happy to think that I could stay in a beach house with him. He had so many toys to play with and his grandmother liked me a lot too. So, I went.

Henry was not a boy I used to play with at school. He was in my classroom and he had a group of friends with whom he played a lot. Some of them were of the bully type but I had never had any problem with them or with Henry. He was the tallest of the group and their leader. He had problems at school and had to repeat one previous school year, so he was one year and a half older than all of us. At that moment in life that makes a big difference. We all were around ten years old, still children, but he seemed to be starting puberty. All my boy classmates were bigger than me and for sure they were stronger too. With any of them, and especially with Henry, I looked like their younger brother. Henry was a very extroverted boy and looked older than his age, not only because of his physical appearance but because of his behavior. He talked about girls and sex as if he were a teenager. However, he was never talking about that in front of any adult.

On the first day at the beach house, I realized we were going to spend most of the time by ourselves. During the day his grandmother was always with us at the beach but once the afternoon was over, we had to stay at the beach house, and we were left on our own. We watched TV, played some portable video games Henry had because his parents had bought them abroad, and I was like in a paradise for kids. When his grandmother went to sleep, she left us in the room we were going to share, and only minutes after she left, Henry locked the door and immediately after that he brought out an adult magazine and opened it to show me. It was a pornographic magazine that I hadn't had any idea existed. Maybe I was too innocent. When I saw the picture of a woman with a penis in her mouth, I didn't understand what that was. I knew about sex, my mother had told me about it, but I had never imagined what I was seeing in those pictures. Henry took his pants and underwear off and showed me his penis as he started to stroke it. I was so confused about what he was doing. He was turned on by looking at the naked women on those pages, showing their breasts, ass, and vagina. I was paralyzed. Looking at Henry masturbating was totally unexpected and unknown to me. Henry told me to do the same as he was doing but I couldn't. He continued and then went to the bathroom for a while and came back minutes later as if nothing had happened. He didn't mention anything about it, and I didn't ask anything too. I didn't know what to think but felt I wanted to leave that house and go back home.

We watched television for a while and then went to sleep. But I couldn't. I was afraid and didn't know exactly why but just didn't like staying there alone with Henry. My mind went wild and up to today I still think why I didn't go out of that bedroom instead of staying with him. I can tell, today, that when I was afraid of something, I was not just scared but terrified. In those

25

situations, I found I couldn't react, and I just get paralyzed and let things happen. That was exactly how I remember it when my father shouted at me and then hit me every time. I didn't run away or hide. Whenever I tried to escape that made things worse with him because one way or the other my father was going to find me or reach me, and I was going to get hit anyway but with more violence. Maybe that was the origin of my submissive personality, maybe it was a decisive part of what caused my shyness and always feeling vulnerable.

When I noticed Henry was finally sleeping, I fell asleep too. A couple of hours later I remember I felt a hand touching me between my legs and I woke up. I tried to move, and my mind was yelling at me to react, but I couldn't. It was dark but I could see Henry had uncovered my legs and had reached my penis with his hand and started to stroke it slowly. I couldn't say a word. I didn't understand what he was doing. I have had erections but had never masturbated before. I didn't know what masturbation was and Henry caused me to get an erection and then he put his lips on my penis and licked it with his tongue. I was scared and paralyzed, again. I tried to close my legs and he pressed very strongly, and it hurt. He looked at me without saying a word but made a gesture with a fist that I should stay quiet or he would hit me. He put my penis into his mouth and sucked it. I can't describe what I was feeling. I have had erections before but have never touched myself for sexual pleasure. I didn't know what sexual pleasure was! It was my first time, and I couldn't believe what was happening. Henry sucked my penis until I remember I felt a sensation running all over from my stomach to my groin like something was going to come out of me. I felt my penis was about to explode and then some sort of contractions took place at the base of my penis that I couldn't control. After four or five of those contractions, Henry left my penis. I didn't understand what had just happened. Now I know I had reached sexual climax and should have ejaculated but that didn't happen. My reproductive organs were still not mature enough and no semen was produced by my body yet.

- You didn't cum. Boys cum, girls don't. You are a little girl. – Henry said. I only looked at him bewildered because I didn't know what was supposed to happen or what did he mean by "boys cum".

- Because you are a girl, maybe you would like this. – he said and took his underwear off standing naked in front of me and masturbating as I could notice in the dark.

- Please, don't hurt me. – was all I said very scared while he laid down by my side on the bed and cuddled me strong from the back, pressing his whole body against mine and I could feel his penis pressing my ass. I started to cry in silence.

- You will like it. – he said and took my underwear down and put his penis between my buttocks probing my ass. I felt his penis reaching my ass hole and suddenly he was like trembling and moaning when moving his hips hard and forward trying to get his penis into me. Before he could do that, he ejaculated on my buttocks. He moved away and turned on the lights.

- You see? Boys cum. I cum over you. – he said and left me there as he went to the bathroom.

I felt his semen drying over my skin. More than innocent, I was too ignorant about sex and went from not knowing almost anything to having my first sexual encounter with a boy when

26

I was around ten years old. What marks, traces, and traumas can this kind of experience cause in a child's mind and heart? I didn't like what happened with Henry that night, but I didn't say anything, I was stunned, scared, afraid. He didn't say anything and went to sleep. I stayed awake for many hours, scared. The next morning, when we woke up, he told me not to say anything to anybody about what he did to me, or he would hurt me seriously.

- From today you are Erica, my girlfriend. And you will do what I want. Ok? – he said and pushed me hard to answer him that I was his girlfriend, or he was going to hit me.

- Yes. I am your girlfriend. – I said lowly, embarrassed and in tears.

We went out of the bedroom to have breakfast with his grandmother who had already prepared everything for us. She asked if we slept well and Henry answered for both of us loudly and with energy, as he was all the time, as if nothing had happened during the night.

I wonder how a boy that was almost twelve years old could have behaved with me the way he did. What experiences he must have had by that time? How were his parents involved in his daily activities and education? How could he manage to get pornographic magazines at that age? Has any adult noticed anything strange about him? He was treated like a prince, being a single child of a rich family, most of the time he was without his parents. Why did my mother leave me with him? I am sure if she suspected a bit of what Henry can do, she would have never left me with him.

That second day at the beach house went completely normal. We played with other boys at the beach, and at the swimming pool, and went sailing on a yacht. I didn't think about what happened the previous night and Henry and I were playing as we usually had done before. At the end of the afternoon, his grandmother had to leave us for a while to buy some food and was going to bring some other boys from the neighborhood to play with us the rest of the day. Immediately after she left, Henry said he wanted to play something with me and asked me to follow him. He took me to a different bedroom, not the one in which we were sleeping.

- This bedroom was used by my cousins when they stayed over. I think we can find something for us to play here. – he said and opened a closet. The closet seemed to be full of some costumes for children. He said his grandmother had that closet so Henry's cousins can have fun wearing costumes at carnival parties at the beach. He asked me to pick a costume and wear it. Then I noticed all the costumes were for girls.

- These are costumes for girls. – I said.

- Yes. My cousins are girls. And you are my girl, Erica. – he said.

I felt I was in trouble again and he was going to force me to dress as a girl. I didn't want to do that. I liked to dress as a girl on my own, secretly. I didn't want anybody to see me. That was my secret and just the idea of presenting myself as a girl in front of Henry or anybody else was stressing me to death.

- I don't want to do that, Henry. – I said and was immediately taken by force by him. He held one of my arms behind my back twisting it and it hurt bad.

27

- You do as I say. You are my girl, Erica. – he insisted making pressure on my arm and I tried to free myself but couldn't. He was too strong for me. I began to cry because of the pain, and he released my arm, but I had nowhere to go.

- You cry like a girl, you see? – he said to me. He locked the door of the room and said he would stop bullying me if I dressed as a girl for him only once. I was trapped. I was wishing his grandmother could arrive to save me from him. I had to tell her what was happening. I knew things could go worse if I stayed silent.

I picked one of the costumes without looking much at it. In another situation, I would have enjoyed wearing all of them. But I was being forced and I didn't like that. I slipped into a sort of yellow party dress that needed to be zipped from the back and I couldn't do that by myself. Henry left the door and came closer to help me. He zipped the dress and there I was, dressed as a girl in front of him. This was a completely different experience from the one with Patty's party dress when I helped my mother. In front of Henry, I felt embarrassed and humiliated.

- You are my pretty girl, Erica. – he said and asked me to twirl for him like a girl. I felt ashamed and couldn't enjoy wearing that beautiful dress, but I made a fast twirl and then I heard that Henry's grandmother had arrived and was calling us. There were more people with her. She was with other boys. I got scared to be seen dressed like that. I tried taking off the dress, but I couldn't unzip it on my own. I had to ask Henry to help me. He laughed and threatened to leave me dressed as a girl unless I do something else for him before I take the dress off.

- Girls like kissing boys. Kiss me, Erica. – he said and I refused so he made a gesture of opening the door. He looked at me and asked me to kiss him again. I approached my face to his cheek and kissed him there very fast and immediately asked him to help me with the zipper, but he refused again.

- You are my girl, Erica. You must kiss my lips. – he said. I was not going to do that and tried to force taking the dress off me by myself, but I couldn't. He opened the door wide, and I could hear the voices of the boys approaching when Henry yelled where we were.

- Please, Henry. I don't want them to see me dressed as a girl…- I begged him.

- Kiss my lips, Erica, and I promise I will help you. – he insisted.

With no other choice, I finally placed a kiss on Henry's lips. After that, he kept his promise and helped me get the dress off just in time so I could get my clothes on before his grandmother and the other boys arrived. I felt abused and humiliated. I wanted to cry and run away. Why was he doing all that to me? Why couldn't I face him and defend myself? I felt helpless and so vulnerable that I went to the bathroom and cried for a while alone. All that made me feel so bad. I wished I could turn back time and had never gone to that house.

I was obviously not feeling like playing with Henry and the other boys. His grandmother talked to me thinking I was feeling sick. She tried to cheer me up to play with the boys and she was staying close. That helped me to feel at least a bit safe.

We had dinner together with his grandmother and the other boys. We played some Atari video games that were not common to have at that time, but Henry had them. I was only thinking that I should tell his grandmother what was happening to get her help. I was afraid to tell her because she would ask Henry and then he would take reprisal on me. How I wished it could be possible to call my mother to take me from that place. How I wished I could vanish and disappear from that beach house.

The second night went without any incidents with Henry and the same happened for the next two nights. We were again like any kids that were playing together and he didn't bully me anymore. The last day at the beach house was a Saturday. His grandmother reminded us that we were going back home on Sunday and then they were taking me to my house so we should make the most of that last day and enjoy. Everything went normal the whole day. Henry was very friendly and happy with me, teaching me how to play some video games, teaching me to dive into the swimming pool, etc. When we went to sleep, we started a battle of pillows and were having fun and finished that last day. I was not feeling threatened and slept well until something happened very late at night. I felt a hand on my head, something touching my mouth, and heard Henry's voice whispering:

- Open your mouth, Erica.

I opened my eyes and saw his penis in front of my mouth. I tried to move away and he pressed his hand on my head to not let me get away from him. He held my hair and pulled it to make it hurt and dominate me.

- Open your mouth, Erica. – he insisted and I felt the pain in my head if I moved just a bit. Again, the feelings of the first night came back. I was being bullied and abused by a boy that was just a bit older than me, but I couldn't stand up in front of him and fight back. He pulled my hair very strongly and insisted forcing me to open my mouth. Scared, I did it. Then he forced me to take his penis into my mouth and asked me to suck it. I felt part of his penis getting inside my mouth and I moved my head away fighting Henry's attempt. He didn't care and laughed while he was stroking his penis very fast.

- This is what happens when you are a real boy. You cum! – he said at the moment he ejaculated and I managed to move away to not get his semen on my face. He released me and kept laughing when I pushed him and ran out of the bedroom. His grandmother woke up because of the noise we made. When she asked what has happened, Henry said that I had a nightmare and was scared.

- That is not true! He is bullying me! – I said, nervously. Henry looked at me trying to tell me to shut up and don't say anything else to his grandmother. I didn't need to give details. His grandmother warned him seriously. She was very angry with him. She said that if he continued bullying me, she was going to tell his parents to punish him and never let any other friends visit him. I feared Henry would take reprisal on me that night but nothing else happened.

The next day I was taken back to my home. When I saw my mother I was planning to tell her what had happened, but I felt too ashamed and embarrassed. My confusion had grown fast and beyond the dimensions of what I could handle. I was having gender identity issues and a

29

messed up beginning of my sexuality too. The experiences with Henry, the pornographic magazines, having him call me a female name and "his little girl", saying that I didn't cum because I was not a boy, and all the feelings, all that was like a boiling pan in my head and my mother noticed something was happening to me. I told her that I didn't like staying with Henry because he was a bully. I didn't give details to my mother because I was ashamed, but she insisted. I talked to her about the pornographic magazines and how he masturbated in front of me until he ejaculated. My mother was completely angry and deeply worried. I was about to tell her all the details of what he did to me and started to cry. She seemed overwhelmed with just that first part I had told her. I could tell she was feeling guilty for letting me stay with that kind of boy. I didn't say anything else. She immediately phoned Henry's mother although I asked her not to do that because I didn't want problems with Henry once we returned to school. She told me I should not worry about that.

My mother never told me what she talked about with Henry's mother, but the result was that I never visited him again and he was never invited to my house either. We never talked about what happened at that beach house. Once we started school and I met Henry again, he was acting very friendly and not like a bully anymore. Something happened at his house with his parents because he changed his attitude and was not the leader of the other bullies anymore too.

The experience at the beach house was traumatic for me, to say the least. It left profound and indelible marks on my personality. My mother noticed and, even though she didn't tell me, I knew she called my father and got him to visit us and get involved in our education, especially with me, because she was profoundly worried. I hadn't seen my father in many years and there he was picking me up from home and driving me out to have the "father-to-son" conversation that I didn't have before. He preached a long monologue of "what does it mean to be a man". He talked to me about sexuality trying to explain it to me in a way that I could understand when he realized I was completely ignorant and didn't know anything about it. From what my father said to me there were some phrases that I remembered for a long time considering the experience I had with Henry.

- Boys don't let other boys touch their ass or penis.

- Boys have sex with girls and not with other boys.

- Boys never kiss boys.

- Boys never wear dresses, makeup, earrings, or long hair.

- Boys never hit girls.

- If a boy hits you, you hit him back.

- Boys are not afraid and never run away.

- Boys never cry.

And in my head, I was asking myself what I was if I had already had a boy sucking my penis and had him ejaculate on my ass, kiss him on his lips, if I wanted to wear dresses and long hair and I didn't want to be hit by boys and I cry or run away instead of fighting... My father made a

30

big effort to repeat those phrases to be sure I understood what he meant. He was not the kind of father that asked what I thought, what I was feeling. After he left me at home, I had more doubts about myself and thought I needed someone else to talk with. As I couldn't feel my mother would understand me, I kept all my feelings and doubts to myself thinking that I will have to discover the answers on my own.

I had the image of Henry's penis ejaculating in front of me for a long time. I went to the bathroom, locked the door and for the first time in my life, I masturbated the way I saw Henry did. Maybe because I was not under stress or scared like when Henry sucked my penis, I felt pleasure when touching myself and reached the same sensation of a burst in my groin and something that was going to come out of me, burning in the base of my penis. As that first time when he sucked me, I had those contractions that come with ejaculation and was expecting to see my semen coming out of my penis but that didn't happen. I only noticed a very clean and transparent liquid dripping, nothing like what I saw happened with Henry's penis.

- "You don't cum like a boy because you are a girl" – I remembered Henry's words about it and couldn't understand what was happening and thought something had to be wrong with me. I masturbated more times then but although I reached what I could identify as a climax, I did not ejaculate. I was not getting pleasure by touching myself. It was more the frustration that I felt each time it happened and started to dislike it.

I thought that, if I stopped thinking about dressing like a girl and all that happened with Henry including my recent masturbation activity, maybe all will fade away and I could have a "normal" life as a boy. I concluded all those things were contributing to my confusion so stopping all that was going to be good for me. I didn't masturbate again and decided not to dress as a girl again too.

I still found myself willing to dress as a girl whenever my sister was leaving me chances to wear her clothes but decided not to do it. It was not easy but finally, I stopped my desire and after a while, I forgot about it and felt somehow better.

Scottish Skirt Lesson

I don't remember much about my experiences with my grandparents while living with them, besides the common daily routines that we shared. My grandfather was not very talkative so chances to have conversations with him were very few. My grandmother was different, and she was like the leader of that marriage. Because we were living at their house with my mother and my sister, my grandmother felt she had the right to take part in our education. As my mother was very busy working, sometimes Nicole and I were left under our grandmother's care and she used the old punishment and reward education method with us, especially with me.

When our grandmother wanted Nicole and I to get involved in domestic activities like washing dishes, cleaning the house, washing clothes, and cooking, I was not reluctant to do that until I realized Nicole was always trying to avoid her duties and my grandmother was forcing me to do them. I didn't like that but did it sometimes until it was me who was doing most of the domestic tasks that were assigned to Nicole and me.

- It is not fair. You are not doing your tasks and Grandma' is forcing me to do them. – I complained to Nicole one day.

- I am sorry. I can't help you with that. Is not my problem. – she answered ignoring how I felt.

- I will not do your tasks anymore and will tell Mom! – I shouted at her.

- I don't care! – she shouted back to me and pushed me to walk out of her bedroom where we were. My reaction was to push her arms from me, and she shouted as if I had hit her. At that moment our grandmother appeared shouting at me saying I was a coward for hitting a girl.

- It's not like that! She pushed me! I was only trying to get his arms off me! – I complained.

Nicole left at once and my grandmother didn't stop scolding me, yelling, and then slapping me on the butt. I started to cry for pain and frustration.

- And now you cry like a girl? Stop crying! You are a boy! – said my grandmother upset.

I couldn't stop crying and that made her very angry.

- You want to continue crying like a girl? Then you will dress like a girl! – she said and took Nicole's Scottish skirt that was on her bed and forced me to wear it. I was afraid of getting hit again and tried hard to contain my tears. Before I could, my grandmother wrapped the Scottish skirt around my waist and fixed it with a large safety pin.

- You will not take it off until you stop crying! – my grandmother threatened me.

I felt humiliated. She stood in front of me while I was forcing myself to calm down. When she realized I was not crying anymore she took the skirt off me.

- That way you will learn how to respect girls and not hit them. – she said and then left me.

I went to my bedroom and stayed there alone, waiting for my mother to come home. She needed to know what happened and I was sure she was going to help me.

My mother didn't arrive early that day and I couldn't see her until the next morning when we were going to school. I told her I needed to talk to her, and she said it was not necessary because she had already talked to my grandmother.

- Don't worry, sweetheart. That will not happen again, and Nicole will begin doing her tasks as she should.

We didn't talk about that episode again. I don't know if my grandmother told my mother she hit me and forced me to wear a skirt "to teach me how to be a boy". The good thing was that after that day, my grandmother never hit me or punished me in any way and Nicole started doing her tasks at home without complaining.

Growing older, when I was around twelve years old, I was devoting my time to many activities at school and home. I was having a good time and those were the years I started going to parties. Almost every weekend there was a party because of a birthday celebration of some of my school classmates or other friends. I was still a bit shy but had grown up and felt better than before. I had two friends, Lawrence and Andrew, with whom we were spending lots of time at my house or their houses. I was also into sports playing football every weekend, swimming and playing tennis too. I was also playing the guitar and was starting to enjoy learning some rock songs I liked and started to write songs of my own. The situation at home was better too. My mother had a better job managing a boutique and my father was visiting us regularly and providing money. Our basic needs were well covered. We were not living with my grandparents anymore. They had died around a year ago and we were only my mother, Nicole, and me at the house.

Those years before becoming a teenager were the ones I can remember I was not thinking much about my gender identity and sexuality issues, and neither did I think about my past experiences with Henry or my grandmother.

When going to parties I enjoyed being with the girls, dancing with them, talking to them, playing some jokes, and making them laugh. My shyness was not keeping me from having a good time. I found I was getting attention from some girls, especially the ones that stood out for their beauty. Both Lawrence and Andrew always asked me to help them ask a given girl for a dance and let her introduce the other girls they liked because "you are the handsome one" they were always saying. "Girls never say no to you" which was something I hadn't noticed, and I was not doing anything on purpose to get their attention. I was just behaving naturally. "Green eyes and blonde hair, you have what all girls like", my friends were telling me, but I didn't care. I wore my hair at shoulder length at that age, I was thin and used to wear only jeans and black or white T-shirts while my friends were trying to look older by wearing shirts. I was more into trying the rock band look and I liked to present myself that way, feeling comfortable with my appearance.

Everything was going well for me until one day, at a party, Lawrence asked me which girl in our class I liked. Some of them were telling stories about the girls they liked, the girls they have kissed or dated. Andrew pointed out that some girls that liked me were starting to talk about what was happening with me because I had not tried to kiss or ask any of them for a date when it was obvious that I felt attracted to them.

- Don't you like Vanessa? She has a crush on you, it's obvious, and she is gorgeous! – Andrew asked me. I liked Vanessa. She was almost my size, with beautiful dark eyes, and dark hair. She was very talkative and funny too. Although I didn't answer, Andrew realized I liked that girl and insisted that I should tell her. It seemed I was very good at having fun with girls as long as that did not involve moving forward for a romantic relationship because once I knew Vanessa liked me, I couldn't behave naturally as before, and she noticed that.

34

During that party, I danced with many girls but avoided Vanessa because I was feeling uncomfortable knowing she was expecting me to do something else and I felt mentally blocked. Nobody was asking her to dance because my friends had spread the word that I was going to tell her that I loved her. I could not handle the situation. A little bit later, I saw Vanessa dancing with other boys, and she ended up kissing one of them. I felt bad but the worst was yet to come. Another girl approached and told me someone has said something about me to Vanessa.

- Somebody is saying that you don't like girls. Is that true? – she asked me. I was surprised at the question and asked her who had said that. She pointed to a group of boys that were on a corner looking at us. One of them smiled and waved to us. I didn't know who they were but recognized one of those boys was a friend of Henry with whom we played at the beach house almost three years ago. I thought for the first time in more than a year about what happened at the beach house and it was like opening a door that I had already closed. Maybe Henry didn't tell anything to our classmates at school and didn't say a word to me again, but now I was thinking he might have said something to the other boys that were at the beach house and were not from our school. That scared me.

- They say that you like boys. – the girl said.

- That is not true. – I answered feeling very uncomfortable.

- Well, Vanessa thinks it is. She liked you and thought you liked her, but you didn't do anything and now you can tell... – she said, and we saw how Vanessa was kissing that guy she was dancing with.

After a while, Lawrence came to me. He found me angry and worried. I wanted to talk to that boy and ask him why he said that I was gay but decided that was a very bad idea because he could open my experience to more people. I thought the best I could do was leave the party and so I told Lawrence.

- You should have made your move earlier, Eric. I am sorry Vanessa found someone else. – he said with the clear understanding that I was feeling bad for that reason. I was not going to explain anything else to him. I borrowed the house phone and asked my mother to pick me up from the party. Less than an hour later I was back home. When she asked why I wanted to leave the party so early I only said I was feeling tired and didn't say anything else. I went to sleep feeling very afraid of what could happen on Monday at school thinking that maybe someone had shared my experience with Henry at the beach house with more people.

That Monday nothing happened except that Vanessa ignored me completely and some other girls did the same. The boys were not saying anything related to the party. Henry appeared and he was acting completely normal. He did not attend the party and didn't know what happened there with Vanessa and that boy that said I was gay, or so I thought. I didn't ask him if he had told somebody else about what happened at the beach house. I thought the less I talked about all that the sooner it would fade away. I also decided not to go to parties anymore to avoid being exposed to someone. I convinced myself it was better to stay away and alone.

35

I was still invited to parties, but I declined every invitation. Soon, after so many times not accepting an invitation, I was not invited to parties anymore. Through the conversations of my classmates at school I knew there were parties and realized I was not considered to be invited anymore.

- That is what you get because of becoming antisocial. – Lawrence told me. He had insisted many times that I should go to parties and forget about Vanessa. I was not playing football or swimming anymore. I had isolated myself and Lawrence tried a lot to take me out of that mood, but he didn't understand the background and all that was going through my mind. It was not like just going to a party again. It was not that simple. Being alone at home without distractions, without company, and going through mental stress caused the internal conflicts I had with my gender issues and sexuality to reappear. Those days were the most difficult I could remember, and I was experiencing depression.

One Saturday my mother had to take Nicole to a party, and she had to work overtime too. She told me she was going to come late after picking Nicole up from the party, so I was going to stay home alone that night. When she left and I was completely on my own I felt that internal rush I had years ago. My desire of dressing as a girl came back like before. I felt I had to dress again and couldn't stop that feeling. I didn't care about the promise I had made before of not crossdressing anymore.

I immediately ran into my sister's bedroom. I found on Nicole's bed a fashion magazine for teenage girls that my mother used to buy for her. It was a magazine with interviews with artists, fashion, makeup tips, lots of pictures of beautiful teenagers wearing wonderful dresses, miniskirts, bathing suits, personality tests, photos of fashion supermodels, and so many girlie things. I haven't read one of those magazines before as I didn't have any interest in them, but once I opened it and gave a glance at its pages, I was caught by it. What I liked the most was the makeup tricks and tips. There were lessons on how to apply lipstick, mascara, eyeliner, eyeshadows, blush, and more. I stayed quite some time reading it and wanted to take it with me. Then I remembered my mother had a place where she put old newspapers and magazines that she was going to throw away and I found many of those girl's magazines there. I took several of them and hid them in my bedroom in a special place on top of my closet so nobody could reach or find them. Later I developed the habit of reading those magazines every day. More like just reading the magazines it was like studying them. I wanted to know all about fashion and dresses and all about girls' stuff. I realized later that, while my male friends were starting to get pornographic magazines, I was into fashion magazines for teenage girls.

Well, that night I wore my sister's panties again after a long time. I also wore a bra for the first time and put red lipstick on following what I have seen my mother and sister doing and a bit of what I found in that fashion magazine on how to apply lipstick. Looking at myself in the mirror and trying to strike poses like the girls and models in that magazine was a lot of fun. I felt happy again, after so long. I had a big smile on my face again.

As I looked at myself in the mirror and down to the panties I was wearing, I found I was having an erection. Why was that happening? The image of my penis growing behind the silky fabric was something I disliked. I tried to hide my penis between my legs somehow, but it was

36

too late. It was very hard and something sticky moistened my hand when I touched it. I took the panties off and noticed a wet spot on it. My penis was dripping, and it was not urine. I was not going to be able to put those panties back in my sister's drawer. I started to feel very aroused and went to the bathroom still wearing the bra. I remembered my promise of not masturbating again and I didn't want to touch my penis. One of the pictures I remembered from the pornographic magazine that Henry had shown me came to my mind. A man was having sex with a woman but was penetrating her ass. I remember Henry wanted to do that to me, but he ejaculated before he could penetrate me. Thinking of all those things made me feel horny like I had not experienced before. I sat on the floor and probed my ass with my finger and slowly inserted one into my anus and move it in and out and I discovered I felt pleasure by doing that. I inserted a second finger and continued stimulating me and I couldn't believe the pleasure I was getting. I pushed my two fingers as deep as I could and kept moving them in and out as my excitement was growing and increased with every move. Suddenly, I had that known sensation building in my groin, and the base of my penis that was harder than ever. I tried to resist reaching the contractions that I knew were the sign of the climax until I couldn't resist anymore and I saw a big load of semen coming out of my penis for the first time in my life. It was such an incredible and powerful experience. I hadn't touched my penis at all and had ejaculated for the first time. I didn't know that could happen to... boys? Was I really a boy? Why were things happening so differently for me? I cleaned myself amazed at what had happened. Without knowing it, I guess I created a strong mental connection with that experience. Wearing girl clothes was arousing me, and stimulating my anus while being dressed could end in a wonderful climax. I repeated the experience for several days and it became like a pattern: my mother was leaving home with Nicole, I stayed alone, I dress as a girl for some time, and ended with a sexual release by stimulating my anus. This caused me to want to stay at home all the time I could if there were chances to be left alone. During regular days it was not possible but there were chances, especially during weekends when my mother and my sister were both going out. My mother was worried about me because I was not going out with friends, not going to parties, and preferred to stay alone.

- What are you going to do all by yourself at home? - she asked me many times before leaving and with her question my mind was triggered to a daydream about the clothes I was going to wear and to try other things I haven't tried yet like high heels and full makeup for example.

Although the relationship between my habit of wearing girls' clothes and ending with sexual stimulation and the climax was very strong, not whenever I was stimulating my anus could I ejaculate without touching my penis. Those times I ended up masturbating like I remembered Henry did, but I didn't like that. So, my sexual relationship with my will to dress and feeling sexually aroused started to change. In the beginning, my crossdressing habits had nothing to do with sexual activity when I was five years old. I think the next phase I went through was like any teenage boy discovering a way to give pleasure to himself and finding ways to feel better or more pleasure. In my case, that sexual discovery mixed with my desire to crossdress was not the driver and not the reason why I wanted to dress like a girl.

Step by step, the sexual stimulation that dressing had caused me was reducing until a moment came when I was not feeling any sexual arousal when I was dressing as a girl, and I still felt wonderful anyway. My subconscious was driving me more. The sexual pleasure was not something I was looking for. I was looking to find my image as a girl. That was important and key for me and whenever I could do that, it was so gratifying and fulfilling.

Reading the girls' fashion magazine helped me to learn a lot about makeup. I learned about the names of the makeup articles and how to use them and I had the time to try makeup on me sometimes but not completely. It was not easy to achieve good results without having somebody to teach me. I became very interested in seeing my mother or my sister or any women I could see on the street, on TV, or in a movie and tried remembering how they were applying makeup and then trying the same way myself.

Growing into puberty I usually had around four hours on a Saturday night on my own at home at least once every month. My mother continued to be worried about me, but I was happy. I was not sad or depressed as before. Being able to dress as a girl frequently without the risk of being caught was helping me although it was clearly not my reality. I mean, I wanted to be a girl, yes, but I could only dress like one. Was there a solution for that? I kept thinking about what kind of miracle could happen so that one day I could become a girl. Why did my body have to be so different from what I wanted? What could I do to somehow change it? I was thin and most of my sister's clothes and some of my mother's fit me well when I was becoming a teenager. But that was not enough. I let my hair grow a bit longer and tried some feminine hairstyles, but I didn't have girly hips or butt and I was not going to grow breasts. I had started to develop body hair, facial hair, and genital hair, and I disliked it. I was lucky that those hairs were not much and not dark either, so they were not very noticeable when I was dressing. I learned how to hide my penis and got used to tucking it very well even if I was not dressing as a girl. I needed to hide my penis as I didn't like it. By then I have very much disliked touching it and at that time I thought I wanted to have not been born with a penis or wanted to get it removed. Was that possible? If I could get rid of my penis, would it be possible to stop becoming "more male" and have chances to become a girl? Was there any other person like me living a similar situation and having the same feelings? I wished so much I could have somebody to talk to about all my questions and feelings without the fear of being rejected.

I increased my makeup practice, learned how to put on different types of bras, and hair accessories, and tried to learn how to walk in my sister's shoes that had low and medium-height heels. I enjoyed dressing completely and trying different outfits and was feeling so happy and satisfied with the girl image of myself that I was able to achieve. I was trying to be very careful when taking my sister's or mother's clothes and then putting them back without having them notice what I had done. I had grown up but still remembered very well that time my mother almost caught me when I was dressing in Nicole's school uniform, and I didn't want that to happen at all. Today I realize I should have been discovered due to the risks I took. Maybe my mother and my sister suspected but never said anything to me. I was always very careful putting their clothes back as they were in their drawers before I wore them, but there were times they noticed something was out of place and wondered what could have happened. Looking back, I can say I was not as careful as I thought I was and I had some crossdressing experiences that were too risky, taken to the limit. Maybe it was a hidden desire of being discovered?

I was fourteen years old when one day, late at night, I finished studying for an exam I had at school. My mother and sister were already sleeping. I went to the bathroom and found my mother's makeup box there. It was never in that place and I was surprised and excited at the opportunity I had in front of me. I had already tried lipstick and eyeshadow many times before but never tried eyeliner and mascara. There were a lot of other makeup articles and for many, I had a good idea about how to use them based on what I had read in the fashion magazines and seen my mother, sister, and other girls doing. Having the complete makeup box for me was something I couldn't let pass. I didn't think about the possibility of having my mother or sister come to the bathroom that we shared. I locked the door and tried several lipsticks until I found a pink one that I loved. It smelled wonderful and was so soft when applying it. Then I tried eyeliner and that was hard to get done well. Eyeshadows were not that complicated and applying mascara was something that got me very excited because of the feeling when curling my eyelashes with it and because of how it really changed my eyes so much making them look very feminine for me. The overall result maybe was not great but good enough for my first time with full makeup. I was so happy and couldn't stop looking at myself in the mirror and combing my hair trying to give it a girlish look too, as it was long but still not enough as I liked. I found pink nail polish and didn't hesitate in trying it. I had tried it before, and it was something I was not good at, but I worked a way to finish and let my nails dry. All that took me some time, but I had lost track of it. Looking at my face in the mirror wearing full makeup I felt the need for dressing. I put all the makeup articles back in the box and when I was about to leave the bathroom I realized that I was not going to be able to remove my makeup or clean my nails if my mother or sister woke up. I was so excited that I forgot that important fact. I thought I could try washing my face with water and soap but needed polish remover for my nails and that was at my mother's vanity in her bedroom. I didn't know how I was going to do that. Time was passing and there were more chances of having them wake up. Without thinking about it I went to my sister's room first. I entered as quietly as I could and found she had left a white mini skirt and red top on a chair together with her bra and panties. I took all the items carefully trying to remember the way they were on the chair and left her bedroom. She didn't even move, and I felt relieved. I knew I was risking too much but I didn't want to stop. Finally, I went back to the living room where I was studying and dressed there. My sister's clothes fit great. I was still a bit smaller than her by then but not much. I had to fill the bra with my socks to give myself the appearance of having breasts and I loved my look and felt so happy I wanted to walk all over the house dressed that way. I turned off the lights in the living room and walked around the house in joy. I wanted to wear heels but that meant going back to my sister's room and I thought with the heels I couldn't walk without making noise, so I gave up on that. I enjoyed moving around, sitting, walking, practicing feminine gestures, and feeling like the girl I wanted to be. In the middle of all that joy, I heard the door of my mother's bedroom opening. She had woken up to go to the bathroom. I went to the living room silently and took my boy clothes I had left there and stayed in silence and in the dark dressed as a girl searching for a place to hide while trying to see if my mother was going to the bathroom. When I saw she closed the door of the bathroom I walked fast to my bedroom trying not to make noise. I thought of taking off my sister's clothes but had no time. I heard my mother leaving the bathroom and so I threw my clothes into a corner of my bedroom and jumped on my bed dressed as a girl and covered myself pretending to be sleeping. Seconds after, my mother was going back to her bedroom but stopped at mine first and I heard her step in. My heart was beating fast and

39

I thought it was about to explode. I was so scared of being discovered and was almost trying not to breathe to avoid anything that could catch her attention. I imagined her approaching and finding out what I was doing. I imagined she was turning on the lights and asking me to get off the bed and uncover. But I was lucky. As she came in, she left. Maybe she was just wondering if I was sleeping as she knew I was studying late. After she left, I knew it was going to be very difficult to move around to clean my face, get the nail polish remover and put my sister's clothes back in their place without being discovered. I felt trapped while waiting some time for my mother to be sleeping again and was thinking my sister could wake up at any time too and could find her clothes were missing. After a while, without turning on the lights, I changed my clothes and hid the skirt, top, panties, and bra in one of my drawers, and went to the bathroom again. I had to turn on the lights and locked the door to wash my face many times but could always notice traces of eyeliner and mascara remaining. It was very complicated to get my eyes clean again and I understood how important it was to have makeup remover and I had no idea where my mom had hers. When I finished, I went back to my room and took my sister's clothes from my drawer back to her room. I was lucky she didn't wake up and I left everything on the chair as they were before. The last part was to get the nail polish remover from my mom's vanity. I waited for a long time until I decided and got the courage to get into her room. I managed to get it without waking her up and was able to remove the nail polish and went to sleep, finally. While on my bed, I was remembering all that happened and prayed that I could have not forgotten anything and still worried about the black traces of eyeliner and mascara on my eyes. I can't imagine how I took those risks. I guess my need of dressing as a girl to express how I felt at that time was so strong that I just couldn't help it. I had to dress, I had to wear makeup, I had to act feminine... I had to because I loved all that... because it made me feel happy and be me.

The next morning, I washed my face several times and it seemed no makeup traces were left as my mom and sister didn't say anything when they saw me. I was happy. Everything seemed all right. In the afternoon, when we were back from school, my sister was going out with some friends. She asked my mother if she had seen her pink lipstick. My mother said she had seen it in her makeup box. I was listening to the conversation and trying to follow them to be sure there was nothing wrong that could involve me. My sister said her lipstick was not in my mother's makeup box and I felt worried. I was sure I had put it back in its place. Maybe she was talking about another lipstick, I thought, so I should not worry. I was in my bedroom and took off my school uniform to put on my regular boy clothes, the ones I used the day before, and when I put my hand into one of the pockets of my pants, I found the pink lipstick there. How could that be? Maybe I got so excited that I forgot I put it in my pocket. My sister became angry at not finding her lipstick and my mother told her she had to be careful and not leave her things around. I felt bad and tried to think how I could give it back to her without giving clues about my crossdressing habits. After a few minutes, when she was looking for her lipstick in my mother's bedroom, I rushed into hers, left the lipstick on her vanity, and went to my room. I remember my mother entered my sister's room, saw the lipstick, and told her: "Here it is, at your vanity. You should check better next time". I passed by and looked at my sister's confused face when she joined my mother as she had already checked there and told my mother about it. "It was not there!", she said angrily. My mother tried to finish the conversation by saying: "Anyway, we found it and that's all. I have told you to be careful about where you leave your things. By the way, next time you use my nail polish remover remember to close it properly. It fell off from my vanity today and it spilled a bit on the floor." My sister complained she had not used it and my mother answered: "Ok, maybe it was me who didn't close it well then…, and maybe it was also me who dropped pink nail polish on the floor of the bathroom when I never paint my nails there and you do." I felt deeply bad. My mother and sister were not having the best relationship those days and I was not helping by generating confusion between them. I learned how to be more careful, and how to not leave traces or clues that I was using their makeup and clothes. Of course, I decided to wait for better times to dress to avoid all the rush I went through and could enjoy it fully. I wanted my "girl time" to be fun and not to be stressed hurrying up. Thinking today about this experience and others very similar that happened while living with my mother and sister, I wonder if they were suspecting anything about my crossdressing. It is hard to think they didn't, but maybe they didn't want to ask me as they might have been as scared to discover what I was doing as scared as I was to open my heart to them and share what I felt.

It was almost the end of the year at school and there was a closing ceremony and a party too. All the students were supposed to attend and that was the time to invite someone to the party. I didn't want to go but my mother insisted. At school, all the boys were talking about which girl they were going to invite to the party but not me. I had become distant and spending more time on my own. During those weeks I had to listen many times to some of my friends asking me who I was going to invite to the party. The date was approaching, and I had decided I was not going to the party no matter what.

- Don't you like girls? - I was asked several times when I was young. I was shy and didn't behave like other boys that were looking for girls, but I knew I liked girls. I didn't have a girlfriend as many of my friends and people started to ask me why. Some of them asked me if I was gay and for me, it was the start of more self-questioning. It was very annoying. I realized I had more doubts about my sexuality and gender identity than I could have wanted as a teenager.

One night I thought about all those questions. I couldn't find the answer but concluded something about girls: I liked girls so much that I wanted to be just like them. I was sure nobody was going to understand what I was feeling. I was sure nobody was feeling the way I did and asked myself why I had to be that strange, why I couldn't be like others. My depression and sadness started again. I had been dressing often but it seemed that was not enough. The dresses and makeup were not enough. It was clear that if I continued growing up I was going to become "more male", and I didn't want that. I became a very sad, lonely, and depressed person.

During those times at school, I noticed most of the people referred to men dressed as women in disrespectful ways and even insulted them. From what I had seen, if those men dressing as women were identified, they were treated badly. I didn't want that for me and kept on thinking about that miracle I wished could happen or something not yet discovered that could help people like me. I was wondering about the lives of those who had been brave to move forward and were living presenting themselves the way they wanted, expressing the gender they identify with. How they could be handling so much hostility from society? Is there a way to find happiness when you feel so different and rejected?

41

It was during that time that I read a story of a girl in a James Bond movie that was born a boy. That was the way they presented the article in the newspaper. The story was a couple of years old but for me it was new. I learned about the word transsexual then and I remember asking myself with a deep feeling of hope how a "sex–change" could happen. I was impressed when I saw the picture of the beautiful Caroline Cossey and read about her. I couldn't have known she was born with a male body. The article was not fully detailed about her journey and the struggles she went through, but I could imagine it was not easy and it required a lot of courage to reach the life she wanted. Learning about Caroline Cossey I knew I had to do something about my gender identity issues but didn't know how. My inner struggles were becoming harder and there were times my depression was too deep over the stress of not feeling able to come out to my family. Dressing when I could was something that helped me to ease that stress sometimes, at least a bit. But the truth was I was growing older, my body and face were becoming more masculine, and I didn't like it. I needed help, desperately.

Looking at the pictures of Caroline Cossey made a big impression on me. I cut her pictures from the newspaper and kept them hidden for myself. She was so beautiful and sexy, especially in her photos wearing a bikini and lingerie. She had become one of the most beautiful women I had ever seen, and I wanted to be like her so much.

I wanted to look at myself in a bikini but neither Nicole nor my mom were wearing bikinis to the beach, so I was not able to try wearing that type of female bathing suit at home. Looking at Caroline Cossey's photo in black lingerie made me want to try that look.

I had never tried dressing only in lingerie to see how I could look. To model lingerie as Caroline Cossey in her photo I needed a black silky bra with matching panties and black stockings with garter belts. My sister didn't have that, so I was going to have to look for them from my mother. That was more difficult because her room was not close to mine. Finding a way to sneak into my mother's lingerie or other stuff was most of the time not possible during the daytime. One day I got the chance while she was taking a shower at night. I was able to get the black silky bra and panties and the black stockings too. I didn't find the garter belts, but I was happy with what I had already found and went to my bedroom. I was getting too excited at the idea of wearing that lingerie that I didn't think about how to put them back later considering my mother and Nicole were at home. When I was about to try them on in my bedroom, Nicole knocked at my door. I had to hide the lingerie in my school bag and opened the door. She said my mother wanted me to wash the dishes in the kitchen that night because Nicole had done it the last time. I couldn't dress in the lingerie and after I finished at the kitchen and went back to my bedroom, my mother came in. She wanted to talk to me about something important, she said. I immediately thought she had found her lingerie was missing. How could I have been so dumb to take them with me while she was at home?

- Are you ok? – she asked me.

- Yes. – I answered wishing deeply she hadn't noticed her missing lingerie.

- I have noticed you are very distant. You look worried and sad. Are you ok? Is there anything you want to tell me? You know you can trust me, sweetheart. I can help you with whatever you need, you know, don't you? – she said lovingly while sitting on my bed at my side. I was sure she had noticed something about my crossdressing habits and was about to open the conversation with me. I looked down to the floor trying to hide my face as I felt tears were going to come out of my eyes.

- I am ok, Mom. Everything is ok. – I answered knowing that was not what I wanted to say. She raised my face with her hand and looked into my eyes wondering what could be troubling

43

me. I held my tears as I was not feeling I could tell her anything about my thoughts and desires of wanting to become a woman, but my resistance was reaching its limit.

She insisted and I stayed in silence waiting for her to open the crossdressing conversation when she said that maybe because I was becoming a teenager I was having some concerns, some questions about sexuality, women, and men's stuff that I might feel better to talk with a man and not with her. I felt relieved but also disappointed. She suggested I talk with my father, but I didn't want to. She asked me if there was another man in the family that I may consider I can talk to about all that because it was an important thing to do at my age. I answered there was none and to finish the conversation I said I would think about talking to my father. She didn't insist anymore and changed the topic. We ended up talking about other things for a long time until she left me in my bedroom and went to sleep.

The next day when I was at school and opened my bag to take out a notebook, I realized I had my mother's black lingerie there with me. Because of the long conversation with my mother the previous night, I forgot about the lingerie and now I had her bra, panties, and stockings there in my bag at school. I became nervous at the thought that somebody could discover what I had there. Why was a boy taking female underwear to school? I had seen many times how boys or girls in my classroom were playing jokes on some students hiding stuff in the bags of others when nobody was looking. I didn't want to imagine somebody trying to hide something in my bag and end up finding the lingerie there. At recess, I took my bag with me and went to the bathroom. I thought the best way to hide them could be not having them in my bag and I could wear the stockings and panties under my school uniform, but I doubted I could do that with the bra as I was afraid the straps would be noticed at my back even if having my school jacket on. The thought of having the lingerie found in my bag or having somebody find out I was wearing them was equally frightening. Throwing the lingerie away was not an option as my mother could notice later that it was missing. From the different alternatives I thought, having the clothes with me under my school uniform was less risky if I was as careful as I could be. At that moment I also felt a rush and compelling desire to wear the lingerie, losing perspective of where I was and what could happen. I guess I was out of my mind and am still surprised today by what I did. I put on the panties, stockings, and bra under my school uniform, and wore a sweater and a jacket on it to avoid as much as possible having the bra to be noticed. I went back to my classroom and stayed put in my place for the rest of the day, thinking of how good it was to be wearing lingerie. Before the last class was over, I needed to go to the bathroom. I had been holding on to my need to pee but couldn't last any longer and had to leave the classroom. When I was there, the bell rang, the school day was over, and I went back to my classroom to pick up my bag and leave. Most of the students had already left. I picked up my bag, went back to the bathroom, and decided to take off the lingerie and put it in my bag before going home. I thought I had been very lucky the whole day for not being discovered and still had to go home and find a way to put my mother's lingerie back into her drawers. When I was putting the lingerie in my bag, I found something in it that was not familiar. It was a magazine. I took it out and it was a Playboy magazine somebody had put in

44

my bag to hide it. I had been very lucky, very lucky indeed. If I would have left the lingerie in my bag, somebody would have found it.

I was curious about the Playboy magazine. Since that experience with Henry at the beach house when he showed me a pornographic magazine, I had never had one in my hands. I was curious about what was special in that magazine that all boys were talking about so much and getting turned on as they were saying. I opened the magazine and glanced at it. Their pages were full of mostly naked women showing their whole bodies in sexy positions. I couldn't deny they were gorgeous and very beautiful. But I couldn't get why looking at women like them was turning men on so much. There were other women dressed in very sensual lingerie that left their intimate parts exposed, and I found them not as nasty as the photos Henry showed me years before. They were very beautiful and sexy photos, but I was not turned on. I left the magazine there in the bathroom and went out. If the next day I was asked, I would just say that I didn't find it in my bag, that maybe somebody else moved it.

At home I had trouble putting my mother's lingerie back into her drawers but managed to do it without having her notice they were missing or asking about them. I had missed my chance to wear lingerie like Caroline Cossey in the photo of her that I had and look at myself in a mirror. I didn't enjoy wearing lingerie under my school uniform and didn't do that ever again. For me, it was not fulfilling to wear a piece of female clothing under my male clothing. That was not giving me thrills at all. Not being able to dress as I wanted always left me feeling empty and discouraged.

Night At Johnny's

One weekend I was invited to sleep over at a school friend's house. He was Johnny, a guy that studied at my school only that year. His father was a diplomat, and they were staying in my hometown only at that time. We became good friends and I had not been visiting anyone but this time he asked me to stay overnight. Since he was a new friend, I accepted.

Johnny was a good guy. He had two sisters, Stephanie and Christine and we spent time together having fun. We rode bikes at the park, swam in the swimming pool they had in the house, played video games on his Atari, watched movies on their brand-new Betamax, and had pizza for dinner. It was a great day. Christine was older than Johnny and I and did not stay much time with us. Veronica was two years younger than us and almost stayed the whole time with Johnny and me. She was very funny, and it was great to stay with her too.

When it was time to sleep, Johnny told me there was a bedroom for me. His house was so big and had two bedrooms for guests. He took me to the one I was going to use. When he opened the door and walked in with me, I felt like I was in an expensive hotel. The bedroom was double the size of my bedroom at home and it was carpeted. I was impressed. The bed was also larger than mine and it was looking so comfortable. After that Johnny told me where the bathroom was and said goodbye. Just before he left, Stephanie arrived. She wanted to say goodnight to me too. She was wearing a cute floral nightie. We said goodbye to each other, and Stephanie surprised us kissing me on my cheek, and then ran away fast.

- She likes you. – Johnny said smiling at me.

- She is cute and funny. - I said.

- I am serious. She told me she likes you. – he remarked.

I only smiled. Stephanie was nice and cute, but I could see her only as a little sister. Johnny left and I prepared to go to sleep.

It had been a very long day full of activity and I was tired. I closed and locked the door to change my clothes, wore pajamas, and went to sleep. When I was on the bed and turned off the lights, I thought if I knew I was going to sleep alone in a bedroom I could have brought with me lingerie and a nightie of my sister to spend the night like a girl. I imagined sleeping dressed as a girl and how it could be. Stephanie came to my mind too. If she liked me and had told Johnny about that, she may be expecting something from me. For a minute I thought maybe she could be my girlfriend and maybe that could help me with my gender identity and sexuality issues. I felt sorry for thinking that way. It was not fair to involve Stephanie or any other girl in my confusion. Those thoughts stayed in my mind until I fell asleep.

It was midnight when I woke up to use the bathroom. The house was in silence, everyone was sleeping. It was a calm and quiet night. I went back to my bedroom and closed the door. Before going to bed, I looked at the big closet that was there and got curious to see what was inside it. If it was a bedroom for guests, I thought the closet and its drawers would be empty, but they were not. I was surprised to find many things inside, including some clothes and shoes that seemed to belong to Johnny's father. I searched hoping to find some female clothes until I finally found only one drawer containing female underwear. I picked white panties, and a white bra, and found a white nightie too. Given the size of the clothes, I thought they might belong to Johnny's mother. She was taller than me but was not a big woman. Her panties and bra fit well enough on me. The nightie was a bit large, but I was happy to have the chance to wear it.

I turned off the lights and went back to my bed to sleep with a beautiful sensation of happiness, calm, and freedom, amazed at the chance to be able to spend a whole night dressed as a girl.

That night I slept like a baby. For once, I was not rushing or worried about being discovered while enjoying being dressed as a girl. And that was a wonderful feeling.

As my parents divorced when I was five years old, my mother thought it was going to be good for me to see a psychologist to help me with that family-breaking event. She was sure my sadness and depression as a teenager were because of the divorce. Maybe that was part of it, but I am sure it was not just because of that.

Except for that visit to Johnny's house, I was pretty much alone most of the time not taking friends home or going to study with them at their houses, or hanging out on weekends as my sister was doing. Some childhood friends were still around but we were not together as before. Those days I used to spend lots of time alone, studying, reading, and writing a diary with my thoughts and experiences. I wrote about my gender identity issues too as I was feeling very confused at that time. It helped me to bring feelings and thoughts out of me even if I couldn't reach any conclusions and, many times, I spent hours writing more than reading. I also could spend hours listening to music alone without doing anything. I was starting a collection of some records and I didn't realize, until a friend told me, that I was mostly buying records of female singers. Now I know I identified with them, and it was not just that I liked their music.

I was slim, had long hair and sometimes I wore tighter jeans than were worn by boys back then which made me look a bit feminine. My father disliked my appearance completely and my mother thought something was wrong with me. She expected me to be different at that age and was worried as I was staying at home "too much" and on my own. Staying alone at home meant I could dress as a girl and I took every chance I could for that, but it was not only because of that. I can't explain it, but it was just that I wanted to be by myself.

My mother suggested I should have therapy with a psychologist, but I didn't want to. She insisted that maybe I had some hidden childhood trauma because of my father leaving us and the emotional impact was just appearing. She didn't mention the psychologist could help me with what happened with Henry, but I believed she had thought about that too. I ended up accepting.

While I went to the psychologist for several sessions, I didn't talk to him about my gender identity issues because I thought he could tell my mother. It was helpful talking to him, and I knew he was sure I was not telling all I was going through. We had those Q&A drills where he was asking and I had to answer fast and short and it became obvious that when his questions were related to sexual behaviors, preferences, and gender-related expressions, I couldn't answer clearly and fast. By the way he looked at how uncomfortable I was, he asked me if I wanted to continue. "It's ok if you don't want to", he said. I didn't want to continue but I didn't want to leave him with the impression he was getting that I had some trouble with my sexuality and gender identity. We continued for a while and I tried hard to think fast enough to give answers that could alter his impressions. Today I believe it was very naive of me to consider I could confuse the psychologist with my answers trying to hide what was going on inside myself. And so, he finally asked a question I will never forget: "If you could choose, would you rather be a female instead of a male?" I was opening my mouth to answer my truth but then stopped for a second

48

to give my mind the chance to force a different answer. I stayed in silence as I couldn't speak. He didn't say a word and immediately asked something completely irrelevant to change the topic and finish the session. I was supposed to go again with him, but I didn't. That was the last time.

Maybe he was someone I could have trusted but I decided not to open myself to him. I was too afraid. However, I believe he got a clear picture of what was happening to me. Later I wished I could have opened up to him. Today I am sure many things could have changed at that moment but what happened went in a completely different direction. I didn't open up to him and something strange occurred. I started to develop a strong phase of denial about my gender identity feelings. After that last session I decided I would not go for more therapy and, in an attempt to find a "solution" for my gender issues by myself, I promised, once more, I would never crossdress again.

I persuaded myself that if I stopped crossdressing my desire of being a girl would go away. I managed to keep my promise and even got to feel somehow good about it, or maybe just made myself believe I felt good. I thought I had finally found a way to "clean" my mind and grow up without the need for a psychologist. After a while, my thoughts about gender issues seemed to have been very well suppressed. My sexuality issues were well "covered", or so I thought, but not much later the voice of my "inner girl" proved to me I was wrong.

When that school year was over, I started another summer vacation and was happy again. I got involved with some friends in my neighborhood and, as we were often going to the beach, I was distracted and enjoyed time with them. I was not feeling depressed anymore, I made new friends at the beach and, again, all my gender identity and sexuality issues seemed to have been overcome.

Summer vacations as a teenager were always amazing. We lived near the sea, and we used to go to the beach almost daily and had a lot of fun with our group of friends. I remember one of the girls who was always wearing floral bathing suits. Her name was Veronica. All the boys talked about how beautiful she was. Some couldn't stop staring at her moving around in her colorful floral bathing suit and she seemed to enjoy the attention. I was looking at Veronica wondering what she could be feeling by getting all that attention and, unexpectedly, found myself daydreaming about wearing a bathing suit like hers. I had not thought about dressing in girl clothes for months, but there it was, my inner voice trying to let me know that, no matter how hard I was trying to forget and ignore it, it was going to come back. A friend said to me: "You are hypnotized by her!" and laughed when he found me looking at the beautiful Veronica. I smiled in acceptance. I was hypnotized by her, yes, but not in the way he meant.

It is said that we attract what we think and wish, and I believe it is true. What happens is that we don't always notice it. Sooner or later, it happens, somehow.

One day we had a party at Veronica's house after we all stayed the whole day at the beach. I was still wearing shorts but had taken other clothes with me for the party and wanted to take a shower to change as some other boys and girls did. When it was my turn to shower, I got into the bathroom and closed the door to immediately find several girls' bathing suits hanging there to dry, including the one-piece floral one of Veronica that was always catching everyone's attention at the beach. All the colorful girl's bathing suits were like shining in front of me. It was a temptation I couldn't resist. So many beautiful bikinis and one-piece bathing suits to try! I didn't have much time but enjoyed trying as many as I could in the shower. I liked how some of them looked on me, but what I remember the most of that day was the feeling of the fabric of those girls' bathing suits getting wet on my body while I was showering and fantasizing about being one of the girls at the beach.

After that experience with bathing suits, my "inner girl" had awakened again and it seemed she had decided to prove to me that I was not going to be able to force her back into oblivion once more. Had I forgotten my promise again? I couldn't help it and had to break it once more.

I let my hair grow longer, a bit past my shoulders and starting to reach my back, and let my nails grow long enough so that I can shape them to give a feminine look to my hands without that being too noticeable. My biggest step was to pierce my ears. I heard some girls said when they had their ears pierced the little hole in their earlobes closed naturally and became unnoticeable when they were not using earrings for some time. I thought I could try that and using a needle that I disinfected with alcohol, I pricked my earlobe. It hurt but not too much. The needle was still at the surface of my skin. I pushed it a bit more until I could feel its tip on the back of my earlobe. That part was painful. I pushed it more and heard like something broke in my ear. It was only the needle completely traversing my earlobe. I had to make it pass through completely leaving a disinfected thread hanging through the hole I had just made on my ear. I repeated the action on my other ear and then cleaned both ears with cotton and alcohol. I saw some traces of blood but there were tiny, nothing to worry about. With both my ears pierced, I tried a couple of golden hoop earrings I had taken from my mother's jewelry box. Those were earrings she was not using, or at least I hadn't seen her using them lately. Standing in front of the mirror in the bathroom I put on the earrings. When I heard the "click" of the little piece of metal securing the earrings in my ears and I moved my head to see the earrings graciously hanging there, I loved the sensation. I felt so girly at that moment. My hair was long enough to comb into a half tail to let my earrings be seen and give my whole head and face a female look. I looked so feminine! It was my first time with earrings, and I didn't want to take them off, ever. I applied red lipstick, eyeliner (which I had already learned how to do very well), and mascara. I added a bit of blush to my cheeks and loved how I looked. I wished I could have had a camera to take some pictures but digital cameras weren't invented yet so I would have needed to take the film to some place to get them developed. I couldn't do that.

I was loving my look and wanted to fully dress but I was not alone. Nicole was staying out that night, but my mother was sleeping. I was taking risks again. It was long since I had dressed fully for the last time and my enthusiasm, joy, and desire to have all those wonderful sensations again were so big and strong that I surrendered to them. I got into my sister's room and found her prom dress in her closet. She had finished school just a couple of months ago and her prom dress, a wonderful turquoise strapless one, was hanging there in her closet. I felt that it was waiting for me since the first time I saw it. I took it carefully to my room and laid it on my bed. I also took the white high heels she wore at her prom party. I had to look for a strapless bra and some nylons to fill them to make my breasts and needed to search in her drawers until I found what I wanted. Being a strapless dress, I had seen girls wearing those dresses and they used a necklace to decorate their necks and chests. I found a golden necklace with a heart pendant. It was going to match my golden earrings perfectly. I was so excited! I found a couple of golden bracelets too and a golden ring. Everything was going to match wonderfully. I couldn't stop looking for what else could I wear to complete my look without overdoing it. I found the nylons I needed for my breasts and finally a pair of skin color pantyhose and white silky panties. When I got back to my room carrying all that stuff, I realized it was risky, far too risky than ever before. For a minute I doubted I could complete doing what I wanted. I wanted to be the girl in the beautiful prom dress. That is what I wanted. There was something stronger than my fears pushing me to continue and I did. I put the white silky panties on after tucking my penis perfectly. It was not noticeable at all, and I loved looking myself down there and finding no bulge. Then I put on the pantyhose, carefully, raising my legs one at a time while sitting on my bed, as I had learned after seeing so many women do it. After that, I put on the strapless bra, and I liked very much how it looked on my thin body and small ribcage. I stuffed it with the nylons to give me the 34B cup size that my sister had so I could fill the bra and the dress properly. I wanted to look at myself in the mirror only in lingerie. I ran to my sister's bedroom where she had her long mirror. I was amazed! I looked so feminine and even sexy! I ran back to my bedroom to finish dressing up. I was so excited. Whenever I was moving fast, I could feel my earrings touching my face and my neck. It might be just a small thing, but I was loving that too. I put the necklace and the bracelet and the ring on one of my fingers on my left hand and I thought of doing my nails, too. They were already long enough and just needed to be well-shaped which I did. I went back to my sister's room once more but didn't know what nail polish color to choose that could match the color of the dress. I found a transparent one that was only going to give my nails some shine and thought that was going to work well. Back in my bedroom, I painted my nails and then had to wait for them to dry. The smell of nail polish has always transported me to all those girlie moments I have had all my life. Wearing only lingerie, I went to my mother's bedroom to confirm that she was fully asleep. She was. She had worked hard and late the previous few days and I was sure she was not going to wake up until morning. I tried to believe that. I went back to my bedroom. My nails were dry and looked perfect and feminine. I took the prom dress from my bed very carefully and slipped into it slowly raising my arms and putting my head into it until it fell to my shoulders and chest. I stretched it to let it lay down fully and I felt my skin covered by the dress and couldn't believe what I was doing. Nicole's prom dress fit very well, almost as if it was made for me. It was a great advantage to be almost the same size as my sister at that time and be thinner than she was. The dress fell almost perfectly from my chest to my waist and down to my legs. I adjusted it well so that my strapless bra was not noticeable at all. I had to zip it from the back but had already learned how to do that on my own and didn't need help. Then I sat down on my bed carefully stretching the dress from the back to not wrinkle it when sitting. I put on the white high heels and stood up. I had worn high heels before but not this size. They were 6" inches heels. It was not easy to walk at first, but I got used to them walking in circles in my bedroom trying not to make noise. I had practiced walking in heels before and focused on first putting the heel on the floor before the tip of the sole. After a little while I could walk decently but knew it was going to require more practice. I was ready, fully dressed, and completely done. I walked to my sister's bedroom to look at myself in her mirror hearing the heels tapping the floor. When I saw my reflection happily smiling like never before in my life I couldn't stop posing and twirling and getting closer to the mirror to look at me and be sure I was not dreaming. "I am a girl," I said repeatedly to myself. I was born to be a girl.

I wanted to go to the living room to walk there as it was the largest room in the house. The sound of my high heels tapping the floor as I left my bedroom could wake up my mother, but my excitement made me forget my mother was sleeping. I had lost track of the time.

I got to the living room walking in the dark and I turned on the lights once I got there. I closed the doors and locked them just in case. The truth was that if my mother appeared and tried to open the door, I would have to face her completely dressed as a girl as there was not going to be any chance to hide or undress at all. I was taking too much risk at that time but my happiness and will to let my "inner girl" express herself couldn't be stopped that night. My last thoughts of resistance and fear were beaten. I accepted that if my mother appeared, I was going to show her who I really was.

Walking there around the living room, practicing my posture on high heels, practicing female mannerisms and gestures, I pretended I was attending the prom party as a girl and something unexpected happened. For the first time, I imagined myself with a man. I imagined I was dancing with him, he was taking me from my waist, driving my steps, getting closer to my body, kissing my cheek, and finally kissing my lips. And I imagined kissing him back as the happiest girl in the world. When I realized I was pretending and imagining being with a man so naturally, I smiled. I felt aroused at the idea and felt my sexual desire growing and liked it so much. I was daydreaming, yes, but for several minutes I had been able to take off to another reality, another dimension, one in which I was a lovely girl that was loved by a wonderful handsome boy. I was hypnotized whenever I looked at my reflection on the mirrors that were there, and by my shadow projected on the walls and the floor. I was in paradise and didn't want that moment to end.

Suddenly, I heard sounds coming from inside the house. I knew it was my mother. I was sure she had woken up and I knew she was going to find out the lights were on in the living room and would come. I had nowhere to go and stayed there. I didn't think of turning off the lights. The time to show my mother my real self had arrived. My heart was beating fast and my anxiety growing at every second. I heard my mother walking. She was going to discover me. I had reached a point of no return and had to face it. Then I saw the front door of the house and had the crazy idea of going out before she could see me. That was not going to solve anything as my mother would find me anyway unless I closed the front door after going out, but I had no key to open it and I would be out on the street dressed as a girl in a prom dress at midnight risking being seen by strangers and who knew what could happen. My mother knocked at the door of the living room and called my name.

- Eric? Is that you? – she asked with a sleepy voice.

- Yes, Mom. – I answered and stood there frozen waiting for her to ask me to open the door that was going to reveal her son as a girl. I had thought about my first sentence to say once she discovered my secret. "Do you remember when you asked me to try Patty's party dress to help you?"

- It's too late, Eric. Go to sleep, sweetheart. – she said and I heard her steps leaving the entrance of the living room and going back to her bedroom without trying to open the door.

53

As incredible as it sounds, the moment of truth was over... without revealing the truth. I stayed frozen for a while thinking about what had just happened. My life was about to completely change, I had accepted being discovered, exposed myself to the limit, and finally, nothing had happened. Instead of making my way back to my bedroom to change into my boy clothes and clean all the makeup and everything, my "inner girl" wanted to raise the bar of risk a little more. I walked to the front door and opened it. It must have been a bit past midnight. I took a step out and then another, holding the door with one of my hands to avoid closing it by mistake. I stood out on the street that summer night looking at the lights of the city, feeling the breeze on my face blowing my dress and my hair. There were flowers on a window a couple of meters away. I wanted to pick one. I left the door and went out to pick a flower hearing my heels tapping the sidewalk. I forgot that the door could close by itself and it was only me, me in the way I dreamed. I walked back to the door and it had not closed. I was lucky, again. I closed my eyes and took a deep breath and smiled smelling the flower when a car passed by. It didn't stop but I imagined I was at the door of my house waiting for my date to take me to the prom party. I imagined he arrived, held my hand, gave me a rose, and took me to dance. I got back inside my house thinking about "him". He was taking me from my waist and walking me into my house. I turned off the lights in the living room, opened that door, walked to my room and so many thoughts were coming to feed my imagination. He was taking me to my room. He took my dress off, my high heels off. He asked me to sit on my bed that gently took off my bra while kissing my neck and touching my body. Then he took off my pantyhose very gently and finally my white silky panties. He pushed me smoothly to lay on my bed and turned off the lights while he opened my legs a bit and lay over my naked body pressing himself over me. He kissed my lips and I said, "I want to make love to you". Then I felt him getting inside me and making love passionately until we both reached an incredible orgasm... What had just happened? Was I in some sort of trance? Had my "inner girl" taken the leading role in my life? I went to the bathroom and looked at myself in the mirror. A happy and naked girl was there. I was there. I had just had an incredible experience pretending a man was making love to me. How would it be if it were for real?

That night was incredible and revealed something of my inner self to me in a way I had not thought or maybe I had but had also denied it. I was not only a girl willing to express herself. I was also a girl willing to be loved and treated lovingly and romantically by a man. Now, some things were making sense to me about my gender identity and sexuality issues. I was a girl and I liked boys. I also liked girls but in a different way. I wanted to be like them.

I managed to put everything back in its place, removed my makeup and nail polish, was sure everything was clean and tidy, and finally went to sleep. I slept well, deeply. I had a dream about what happened that night when my mother was about to discover me dressed as a girl.

- Why are you dressed like a girl, Eric? – she asked me with a smile on her face.

- Because I am a girl, Mom. – I answered her.

- But you are a boy, Eric.

- No, Mom. I am a girl. Look at me. Do you see a boy in me?

54

- It's true, baby. You are a girl, a beautiful girl, sweetheart. – she said and then she kissed and hugged me.

The morning after I woke up later than usual and felt very tired. My mother had left me a note saying she had to pick Nicole up from her sleepover party. I went to the bathroom, sat down to pee (a habit I had been following for several years when not seen in the bathroom), and then washed my head. When I looked at my face for traces of makeup, I didn't find any. I had learned well how to use makeup remover and had one pot of my own hidden in my stuff above my closet to be ready to clean myself anytime. However, when I wet my hair to comb it, I realized I was still wearing the golden hoop earrings. My earlobes were a bit swollen. I took the earrings off easily with no pain at all. I cleaned my little holes with alcohol and then used some ice to reduce the inflammation. After several minutes my earlobes were feeling better. I wondered if it was true that the little holes would close by themselves naturally if I was not using earrings again. I had to try and see how many days that was going to take. In the meantime, I had to be careful to cover my ears with my hair so nobody would notice I had them pierced. Around a week later the holes were closed and nothing was noticeable. There was a very little scar but nothing to worry about.

The next weekend I crossdressed again and wanted to wear earrings. I tried to see if I could find a way to still use the little holes. When I found the exact place where I had pierced my earlobes before and press the pin of the earring, it got in and it was easy to find the way out on the back of my earlobe by pressing a bit more. It caused a bit of pain for a little while and then it passed through. I understood I couldn't do that very often unless I wanted to have permanent noticeable holes. Even though sometimes I did it more often than I thought was safe, nobody told me anything about my pierced ears if they found out.

When I was young there were times I could stay away from dressing as a girl and not even think about it for months but when Halloween was approaching, I couldn't help it and felt that was a chance to take advantage of the situation and go to a party dressed as a female character. I must be honest; I was too shy and too scared and had no confidence to do that because I was thinking somebody could tell that I was enjoying it "way too much" in my disguise. Some of my male friends did go to Halloween parties dressed as females and some girls as males and everyone was having so much fun not seeming to care at all about what anyone was thinking. I never did it. My fears were too big, and the day after I was feeling sad for missing an opportunity to dress as a girl in public.

Sometime later I was invited to a costume party and my group of friends, boys, and girls, were thinking it could be fun if we all went crossdressing. That was one of the ideas and although I saw it as another chance, I was afraid again. I couldn't avoid feeling that way. My friends, especially the girls, got very enthusiastic about the idea of working their makeup skills on us and lending us some of their clothes too. I was thinking about it and exposing myself to have a girlfriend dressing me as a girl was both like a dream come true and my greatest fear of being discovered how much I liked it. Girls could tell, I was sure. Finally, some came up with other ideas and I felt somehow relieved. My closest friends, two boys, and one girl, decided we should go as the rock band Kiss wearing makeup, wigs, platform heels, and all that. I was excited at the idea and I wanted to be the Demon, but my friends said they had already thought about it and I was going to be Starchild as they had already picked their characters. It was going to be a lot of fun, I was sure. It was not crossdressing, so I was not nervous. One of the girls was in charge of our makeup and she did a very good job with my three friends and their looks were amazing. When it was my time she prepared my face, painted it white with the black star on one eye, and then she said, "Lips are the most important part in your case", and started applying the red lipstick on my lips asking me to open my mouth and lift my head just a bit to help her. "You are doing it great", she said smiling and at that moment I realized I was following her instructions very naturally. I had applied lipstick so many times before and knew how to do it well. I pressed my lips together just before she asked me to do that. "You know how to do it, don't you?", she said smiling again and winking an eye. I felt embarrassed and blushed, but she couldn't notice my red cheeks due to the white paint on my face. My friends turned around and looked at me. My fears grew again. I wanted to act as if I didn't care and if I didn't know how to help to get my lips done but I couldn't. "Now put your lips like mine, as if you were kissing, yes, hold it there", she asked me to show how she was doing it. The others started making jokes and I became very shy and she noticed it. She asked them to not disturb or she was not going to finish and we would be late for the party, so they went back to finish their dressing with the rest of their costumes. She looked into my eyes putting her face right in front of me and showed me her lips again. "Kiss the air and hold it there", she said. I did it and when she finished applying the last touches of red lipstick she said: "Perfect! You made my job very easy and your red lips look so kissable now", and she winked an eye at me with an undeniable knowing smile. Girls can always tell. I have no doubt about it.

56

A TV Commercial

There are unforgettable moments that inspired me deeply during the exploration of my gender identity. Remembering what that event or experience caused in me was also relevant for understanding myself, my behavior, and what I really wanted.

I was alone at a retail store and walking near the place where electronic devices were sold. People were walking around checking radios, washing machines, refrigerators, TV sets, etc. I stopped for a while to look at the screen of big screen, of those they called "home theatre". I had never been of the people that watch TV a lot, but just imagining having that big screen at home was amazing. That "home theatre" was surrounded by smaller TV sets and all of them were tuned to the same channel so all the screens were showing the same news program. It was fun to look at all the tv screens changing the images and colors at the same time. Then, a commercial started. A red Lamborghini was stopping at a gas station in a place that looked like the countryside. I haven't seen that commercial before, so I stopped to watch it. Two kids on the grass behind a wooden fence were looking amazed at the impressive sports car and how one of its doors was opening by lifting. I was anxious to see who was going to appear coming out of the car and for a second I thought it would be a man, like a pilot or something like that. When I saw the gorgeous woman wearing a white tank top with denim shorts coming out, turning her head so her wonderful long light brown hair was blown by the wind while she took off her sunglasses and started to walk like in slow motion, I was trapped and couldn't stop watching. She was not just beautiful but so sexy at every movement she did and was only wearing a simple white tank top and denim shorts. I was amazed and it was not only me who was like hypnotized by her image multiplied on all the tv screens around. I was sure who she was. Many people, men, and women had stopped to watch the commercial. When the image of the sexy woman was shown closer, as she was moving her head in a very sexy manner trying to take her gorgeous long hair from her face, I confirmed I was not wrong. She was Cindy Crawford, the first supermodel I felt more than just attracted to. I fell in love with her femininity, sexiness, class, and elegance. Everything about her was inspiring my own feminine identity. When I was a kid, I thought that once I was growing up and become a girl, nobody would tell me I can't wear female dresses and I could be a model.

Cindy Crawford was an icon of beauty during the golden era of supermodels. I had not many sources from where I could get pictures or watch her modeling, but whenever I could find a picture of her in a magazine or a newspaper, I was like bewitched staring at her, looking at every detail of her lips, cheeks, eyes, eyebrows, gorgeous hair, and her mole that became like her signature beauty mark. Many of the makeup looks I tried back then were inspired by the images I had seen of Cindy Crawford. During those days, if I had the chance to watch her modeling on TV in a fashion show, it was a gift to me, and I dreamed of being on stage modeling like her.

When the Pepsi commercial had finished, I looked around and it was obvious that most men felt attracted to it. I could see more men than women stopped to watch it. Each one may have had their reason or motivation. Maybe many decided to drink Pepsi from that day on! That was not my case. I am sorry, Pepsi. For me, I took the image of Cindy as how a woman can be beautiful and sexy with just the way she projects her image, not the image itself. Wearing simple or sophisticated clothes and makeup meant nothing if there is no genuine attitude coming from the inside. What stayed with me was mainly how Cindy's beauty was driven by her attitude at enjoying being her and enjoying what she was doing..., and it also stayed with me the beautiful long hoop golden earrings she was wearing that became my favorite.

Well, I will admit that a bit later, when I watched Cindy Crawford in a Revlon lipstick commercial, I couldn't help to run into a makeup store to buy one for myself and enjoyed so much trying it at home. That was the first lipstick ever that I bought for me. Girls have the prerogative to have a little fun and... Oh oh oh, go totally crazy, as Shania Twain sings, right?

I was almost seventeen and about to finish school. During the past two years, I continued crossdressing, practicing makeup, reading fashion magazines for girls, and have started getting some money in eventual part-time jobs helping some younger students prepare for their exams. I was not the best at school but good enough and I liked the chance to teach. Some students were coming home on weekends so I could help them with mathematics, science, history, literature, etc. I was getting paid and that was enough for me to have some money of my own I could use. Most of that money was for buying records of the artists and bands I liked. I became into rock music and some pop music too. I also discovered country music and loved it making it my favorite. But country music was not the type of music that was most listened in the radio in my country and it was hard to find records in the stores. I was playing guitar pretty well and writing songs. Music was very key for me since I was a teenager and I loved what it generated in me. I thought then that I could become a musician after school. I didn't have a band or had played guitar with others except for very few times but the feeling and will to do something with music was there.

Months before my graduation from school my father and my mother, one at a time, were asking me about what I wanted to study after school, what profession I would like to follow, and what university I was planning to go to. I was not sure what to say. My sister Nicole was already studying at the university to become a lawyer. My mother had no profession, and my father was an engineer. They were trying to show me the importance of choosing the "right" university for the "right" career and it was obvious they wanted me to become a professional.

- You must think about the things you like. All the things that make you feel passionate are a good sign of what you could choose as a career so you can enjoy it and be a great professional because you will be working on what you like to do. – said, my mother. I thought what she was saying was right and made sense to me.

- You must think about the professions in which men are making more money today. You can't choose a career just because it is something you like. You are going to make a living because of working in that career, so you'd better choose well. – said my father from his very predictable perspective.

If I had to think about things I like, then when thinking about my mother's statement about my professional future I should be choosing to become a makeup artist or dress designer, or a musician or a writer. If I let my mind go beyond that, I had imagined I could still find a way to become a woman and make my way in life as a supermodel. I would love to be modeling clothes, lingerie, shoes, bathing suits, etc. That was what I dreamed of doing, but I also thought it was impossible. If I had to think the way my father was doing, then I would need to be born again and there is no way I could take that approach for my life. That was how I was thinking then.

I said to my parents I wanted to be a musician or a writer, but they didn't agree. Time was passing and I needed to decide before the end of the year. I felt I was pushed because my parents were worried that I could finish school and may decide not to study anything and to try to be a musician.

- Eric, you are good at math. You even teach students. Your father and I think you could study engineering as he did. So, you will be able to follow him in the future and work together taking advantage of his connections and the success he has achieved. You can take music as a hobby and later, once you have graduated, you can study to be a musician if you still want to do that.

The words of my mother were not that convincing to me, but I understood the point. My father was not going to support me if I decided to be a musician. I liked engineering because it had to do with technology and that was something I had been interested in, but I was not sure whether it would be fulfilling. The truth is I was not sure but ended up accepting their suggestion. After summer vacation I was going to study engineering at the university.

At the university, things changed for me completely. I had to be so involved in my studies that I had no time for other things. Naturally, I distanced myself from my crossdressing without thinking about it for years. I made new friends, got involved in outdoor activities whenever I could, and I also forgot about becoming a musician or my desire to one day live as a woman. It was like I had moved my interests in the opposite direction.

Being out and far from friends at school helped me, I think, to have a new start. I went to parties, start dating some girls, had a couple of girlfriends, and had sex with a girl for the first time. If I compare my life at the beginning of university with that one at school, it was like the life of a different person. At the university, I became more confident and was not shy anymore. I started devoting more and more time to sports, especially the extreme ones like skydiving, rafting, trekking, hiking, mountain biking, and surfing. I was going out with friends and on my own. I built a very "male" image of myself and got to feel good and happy.

Extreme sports became an important part of my life during university, and I developed skills to guide people on excursions and outdoor activities. What had happened to my "inner girl"? When I think of those days, I just can't understand how it was that all my desires of being a girl and being with a man were completely gone. As strange as it sounds, during that stage of my life there was no more doubt for me that I liked girls, I loved them, I wanted to have sex with them, and I did not doubt that I was straight. Everything was clear. I had grown up as an adult and had become a standard male making his life the happiest he could imagine. I was still writing and still playing music at home and had no remorse for having that only as a personal hobby.

61

I became an adult being fully involved in extreme sports and graduated as an engineer when I finished studying at the university. The day I finished university was the same day my mother accomplished buying a house. My sister had traveled abroad to continue studying with a scholarship in Spain and I was living with my mother, and she was so happy to finally be able to buy a house of her own.

The day after my graduation we had to move to a new house and leave the old one in which we had lived for so long. My mother told me she had almost emptied the old house but had left there many things to be thrown away and others she didn't know if I wanted to keep. After we moved, I went to the old house to check on those things. I didn't think there was anything that I would want from there as all my stuff was already at the new house.

The living room, dining room, kitchen, and bathroom were empty. My mother's bedroom was also empty and there were several boxes and old furniture in Nicole's former bedroom. My mother seemed to have put there all that she thought was going to be thrown away. My bedroom was also empty.

I opened some of the boxes in Nicole's bedroom and I thought nothing was interesting to be kept. Old stuff, broken stuff of different types, nothing that I wanted, until I opened a very big box that was too heavy to move easily. First, I found a bag that I remembered Nicole used for her makeup. It was full of old makeup articles. I found another one holding my mother's old makeup and some very old fantasy jewelry that I had never seen before. After I took the makeup boxes out, I found lots of clothes of all possible kinds. From some winter coats to bathing suits, going through dresses, skirts, lingerie, blouses sweaters. And there was another box at the bottom that was full of shoes, many pairs, of boots, sandals, high heels... They were old, some of them very old indeed. Lots of the clothes I discovered were not articles that I remember seeing my mother or Nicole wearing before.

As I said before, at that time I was living a life being sure about who I was and what I wanted. I had no doubts about my gender identity or sexuality alike when I was a teenager or as a child. I remembered all those moments I had dressed as a girl in that house, all those moments of happiness when dressed or sadness when I couldn't do it and was stressed and depressed, of living a secret. I left all the stuff in that room and walked around the empty house and finally reached the room we used for storage. There was nothing there except for that big old closet in which I hid once, and I was almost caught by my mother wearing my sister's school uniform when I was five years old. I opened that door, got in, and sat on the floor remembering that moment when I cried sitting and hiding in that place dressed as a girl. Why had all that happened when I was a child? I started thinking about all those memories and recalling all those experiences as flashbacks that were reconnecting with a part of me that had fallen asleep for years. I stood up and tried to find the spot on the door where I remembered writing "I want to be a girl" when I was five years old. That was more than fifteen years ago. I found it. It was still there, and the new owner of the house will find it, but I didn't care. The words were there as if I had written them yesterday. I smiled remembering myself at that age and how I believed that when I was growing up I would become a girl just for the fact of growing up. I left the closet, closed the door, and went to the place in the living room where we had the telephone. It was still there and was working. I called my mother at the new house.

- Hi Mom. I think I am going to stay in the old house tonight and will go home with you tomorrow. – I said.

- Why, Eric? Is there something wrong?

- No. Everything is all right. I found a box full of my old books and stuff from the university and I think I need to check them carefully before throwing them away tomorrow. – I lied to my mom.

- But where are you going to sleep? There is no bed there, sweetheart. – she asked me.

- There is an old couch here, don't worry. I can sleep there. It's going to be only one night.

My mother believed my lie. It was true there was a box with my university stuff but that was not the reason I was deciding to stay. The chance to be completely alone in the house with no possibility of interruption at all and having all that female clothing and articles for me had rung the bell of my "inner girl's" heart and she had awakened and come to life once more.

I hung up the phone and went to Nicole's room thinking about all the time and all the clothes I was going to be able to try.

That day at the old house was a special experience. Nobody was going to come, there was no risk of being seen, I could do whatever I wanted and had all the time I needed. I was alone but a bit nervous though. Several years had passed since I dressed as a girl for the last time and I didn't remember how that last time was. Every time I stopped dressing and then did it again, I had that special moment when I finally realized "I am back." It is not just the female look but the wonderful feeling of recognizing "It's me again" and wishing that moment could last forever. Can that happen again after so long?

There was an old partially broken mirror in the room, not very big but I could use it to apply makeup. I had shaved my face early that morning and my skin was clean. I hadn't thought about it, but I had cut my hair short for the last few years. I regretted having done so as I was not going to be able to give my hair a feminine look by combing it as when I had it long. It was too short. I thought that maybe my mother had a wig or hair extensions in her stuff although I never saw her using those things before. I investigated other boxes for a while and finally, to my surprise, I found an old brown female wig. It was for a short hair look and needed maintenance. I also found a set of false eyelashes and a depilatory cream tube. I had seen my mother using that depilatory cream and found it still had some cream remaining and it was not yet due. I took off my shorts and applied the cream to my legs. I didn't have much hair on my legs, but it was certainly noticeable and was going to ruin my female image. I didn't have hair on my belly and had started to grow hair on my chest recently. It was not much, but I also applied the cream there. Following the instructions, after some given time, I got rid of all my legs and body hair. It

63

was the first time to have my legs hairless since I became a young adult. As a teenager, I didn't need to worry much about it because I grew very little hair there.

Again, I felt nervous that maybe my adult male body was turned a bit more muscular because of the intense sports activities, I had broadened my back and shoulders, and my facial features had become naturally more masculine. It was going to be difficult to make my face look feminine so easily. I was still slim and that was the only thing that made me think that at least several of the clothes would fit me.

Before working on my makeup, I decided to make a selection of the clothes I was going to wear to decide how my makeup would be. There were night dresses, casual dresses, formal skirts, and blouses, so I had to choose well thinking of the look I wanted to produce. After I made my choices, I put the different sets of clothes on the boxes around but separately and on the couch I was going to sleep in. Among them, there was a red stretch minidress that I remember Nicole wore for a party a bit before she traveled abroad. I remembered she looked very sexy in it and she was also wearing red high heels. I looked for them, but they were not there. I found a pair of black high heels that could be used instead. My foot size was longer than when I was a teenager and I was able to use my mother's or sister's shoes without any problem. To my sadness, those high heels were too small and I couldn't wear them. I started from the shoes to see if there were some for my foot size and it was obvious most of them weren't. I only found a couple of sandals with heels that fit me too tight, but I could stand the pressure and wear them. That reduced the chances I had to combine outfits, but it didn't stop me. I tried some clothes very fast and discarded all the ones that didn't fit me well. There were some dresses I couldn't get into and they were so beautiful but there was no way to make them fit. I understood that if I wanted to dress again after that day, I needed to buy my own clothes.

Anyway, I was not going to lose the chance to see if I could still look like a girl the way I did when I was younger. I decided to wear panties, a bra, a denim skirt, a pink crop top, and a pair of ankle leather boots that I unexpectedly found at the end and were almost my size. I hadn't done my makeup yet, but I walked freely around the house very comfortable and at ease with myself. The feelings of joy and happiness that I remembered every time I dressed had returned. I went back to Nicole's room and selected a pink lipstick. I found black eyeliner and shades of gray and black eyeshadow. I had not tried the smokey eye look for a very long time. It took me more time than usual but when I finished and applied mascara, my face had dramatically changed. My "inner girl" was starting to show up again and I got excited about it. I used some face contouring powders and had to work a lot to make my masculine facial features less obvious. It was hard. My face had changed more than I liked but I could still manage to make it look feminine. I knew I would have to learn more about face contouring and concealing makeup techniques. When I was done and looked in the mirror after applying the pink lipstick, I blew a kiss at myself in the mirror. I was there, again. My "inner girl" winked an eye flirtishly. She was awake, really awake. The wig I found was not the type I liked but was better than just showing myself with my short masculine haircut. I washed and dried the wig as I could and after combing it a bit, it was ready. I put it on me, adjusted carefully and I was ready. I was not a musician, but I looked like a rocker girl.

I enjoyed being at home so freely as a girl that time passed by without noticing it. I changed outfits and looks the whole night until I was too tired and fell asleep. I didn't need to rush with things like putting clothes back in drawers, cleaning my makeup in a short time, etc. The next day I knew I was not going to be able to take anything with me and felt a bit sad. I didn't know where I could hide things at the new house. If I was going to start dressing again, I should start buying my own clothes, makeup, and shoes. I wanted to develop my own look.

Female Blue Jeans

After I finished university and while living in the new house with my mother, I was looking for a job and it was taking time to find one. Nicole was not at home anymore and the chances of getting female clothes to dress were none. I had to buy female clothes for myself if I wanted to dress like a woman. I had some money but I needed to get the courage to buy woman's clothes and makeup in person. Those were not the times of online purchasing. It is funny to remember the first piece of female clothing that I bought for me was unintentional.

I went to a store to buy a pair of jeans. I went to the male's section and picked two from a pile that had a label indicating my size. One had a zipper, which was the classic style, and the other had buttons and I liked it, so I tried both in the changing rooms. The one with the zipper didn't fit well. It was too loose. I was still thin and I didn't look good in it even though it was my size. The one with buttons felt different but fit well. I realized its fabric was a stretch type and that made it feel very comfortable. It was a bit tight but not much and the waistline was a bit lower than usual too. I decided to buy it and took it to the cashier, paid, and walking out of the store I passed by the women's section. I saw a pile of jeans and found the ones I had just bought for myself. I thought it was strange but maybe mine were the men's kind of the same brand and style unless someone had left one of those women's jeans on the pile of men's jeans from where I took it. I felt strange but also happy about what happened.

At home, I checked the labels of my new blue jeans and I confirmed they were women's jeans, but they fit well, and I decided to wear them. In the end, they were jeans and who would notice, I thought. I went to meet some friends and wore those jeans, but nobody seemed to notice they were female jeans.

One day I met a girl friend at a bus stop. We were very good friends and we used to talk a lot about anything and everything. She looked at me and said: "We are wearing the same pair of jeans" showing me the buttons at the front and twisting her waist a bit to show me the brand at the back of her jeans. "Yes, we are", I answered after realizing she was right and I expected a further comment from her about why I was wearing women's jeans. "Looks good on you", she added, and we continued talking about anything and everything as we always used to.

Half a year after I finished university, I started a job. I had already worked before but this time it was my first official full-time job in my career. At that moment I worked as a technician repairing computers and it was a very demanding job, but I liked it. The money I was getting was enough to help my mother at home while still being able to save some. I couldn't crossdress at home anymore and felt sad about that. My desires were back but I couldn't do anything, not while living with my mother. I wanted to move and live on my own as soon as I could.

In the first years, I didn't crossdress at all and that was generating some stress, but I continued with my extreme sports activities and got distracted. As time was passing by, I was getting more and more involved in those activities every chance I had after work. When I had the chance to take a month of vacation it was unbelievable all that I did. I believe I needed adrenaline in my life. I forgot about music, forgot about gender issues, I was passionate about living my career and extreme sports. When I finally got a way to rent a very small apartment to live independently, crossdressing was not on my mind anymore. It seemed those desires were far in the past once more.

I was meeting new people, going to parties, dating girls, and falling in love with some of them. I felt happy and not stressed, not looking back to the issues of my past at all. I had a girlfriend named Eva. We became very good friends when we met at a party and, after having a couple of dates, we became lovers and had a great relationship. Ironically, she didn't like sports at all, but it didn't stop us from sharing other experiences. Eva was always asking me why I was so much into practicing extreme sports. Once she said, "You want all that adrenaline in your life because you are running away from something ". I tried explaining it was just something I loved so much but she always insisted. We had a very nice relationship. We could have long conversations about anything and everything. Many times she said that talking to me was for her like talking to another girl. She said she had never met a boy that was so sensitive and insisted that I was running away from something or hiding something from others taking the practice of extreme sports as a kind of cover. At that moment I was not open to my feelings as before and the conversations were closed without further thought from my side. Maybe Eva was right and noticed something about me others didn't. I have had sex with some girls, but she was the first girl with whom I made love and we believed we were going to last forever. None of us were thinking of marriage but we wanted to live together, travel the world, and maybe have children after a few years. Things went differently in the end. We split although we stayed friends. I guess we were too much of good friends, I don't know. When I remember those times I had with her, we were very different in many things that interested each other but we were the kind of people that liked to be independent.

I was feeling comfortable with myself and having a life like many other men, enjoying love, sex, hobbies, a job, living on my own, and traveling.

Time later I fell in love with another girl, Maggie, and we started a very romantic and stable relationship. My experience with her was different and very soon we were talking about making plans to marry but we were not living together yet. It was strange that I was thinking and feeling that way. Some of my friends were telling me that I had changed and in some way it was true. I was not as active in extreme sports as before; I was very focused on my job and all the spare time I could have was spent with Maggie. She was a very conservative person and was raised in a Catholic family. I was also raised in a Catholic family but was not into religion myself. She was. I started attending Mass with her and felt good about it. Maybe I wouldn't have gone back to religion if it was not because of her. I didn't realize how much I was changing but I was feeling happy with her and with my life. Professionally speaking my development was good and I started getting more money and was able to move to another apartment in which I was going to live with Maggie once we were married.

During all that, the times of Internet began for me and it was something amazing to discover. It was not the time of Google but of Yahoo, Hotmail, GeoCities, ICQ, and Virtual Places. What an incredible way to get in contact with people and a source of information on any topic I could think of.

Browsing directories in Yahoo I came across a link about "Alternative lifestyles". I had no idea what I was going to find there and was surprised at where that link took me. I found plenty of information about crossdressing and it was far more than I could have imagined. I remember finding a website that was a directory of websites of crossdressers / transvestites / transsexuals from all over the world and sorted by country. What happened next was inevitable. All the years I was suppressing my gender issues were proved to have not been enough to bury them. They all came back and were stronger. I did a lot of searching for information learning all I could. I read about the differences between a crossdresser, transvestite, transgender, transsexual, etc. It was a whole new universe for me. I created an account in Virtual Places with a female name and had my first experiences chatting as a "girl" with other people, men or women. It was very interesting to play the role of a girl and interact with people. For them, I was just an avatar with the name of a girl, and for me, they were the same. Whoever was behind the keyboard could have played the role of anybody, faking their name, gender, and life, and nobody seemed to care much and just had fun pretending to be whomever they wanted to be. The anonymity of the Internet was causing many people to express themselves openly without restrictions. I took part in a chatroom for crossdressers and made some very good friends and for the first time had the chance to talk with somebody about my gender issues, my sexuality, my preferences, and share experiences. I also found some websites where psychologists were sharing their points of view about all that mattered to me related to gender identity. Some terms were different from what they are today. I learned about Gender Dysphoria and understood immediately its meaning and I believed that was what was happening to me. It was a large source of information that I read. I remember other sites with information about transgender-friendly resources for online shopping which I found great to help understand the different clothing articles that were offered for crossdressers. I also found a site with a "gender test" named COGIATI that was intended to help self-diagnosing if you were transsexual or not. Later I found information about that test was lacking scientific and professional authentication but at the moment I found it, it was the first type of online test that could give me an idea of what was going on with me with my gender issues and made me think about myself in a different way. It was like I was doing something to understand myself. So, I took it. The results of the test were showing me that I was very likely to be a transsexual and that I should seek help. I believed it was easy to fake answers to drive the results intentionally, but I answered as openly and honestly as I could. The COGIATI was only in English at that time, and I decided I could do something to have it in Spanish too, my mother language, with the hope that it could be useful for other persons of Latin American countries with gender issues like me. By then I had opened an account on Yahoo under the name of Valeria Carrera, a name I took after the Argentinian supermodel Valeria Mazza, who was very popular then, and Carrera because of the last name of a girl classmate at school that I always liked very much. I wrote an email to Jennifer Diane Reitz, the owner of the website hosting the COGIATI test, asking her permission to translate her COGIATI into Spanish. After getting her approval I felt very encouraged and I worked on the translation for several days. It was not easy because I had to study to find the proper words to use in Spanish and that research helped me understand more and more about "trans people" and about me. After I finished and the Spanish version of COGIATI was online I was very happy and felt I had contributed, at least a bit, to let others have information that may help them in their research in Spanish.

I continued researching, making friends online, and in that way opened accounts on some websites that were like the social networks that we have today. I interacted with people from so many different countries and understood that there were a lot of human beings feeling the same way I was feeling. On one side that was relieving, feeling that I was not alone, but on the other side it was also sad to realize that we are so many but very few of us have been able to move forward in life living the gender we identify with and how much suffering, how little understanding, how much abuse, how little tolerance, how little love existed.

At a given point during that time, I was so entertained with my research about gender identity that it seemed to have encouraged me to crossdress again, but I felt puzzled. I was planning to get married, living alone, had no female clothes around, and had to buy my own. That was difficult, but I did it. I was afraid of being discovered that I was buying girl clothes for me and there were many things I was too afraid to try buying in person like lingerie, high heels, and makeup. My heart was beating so hard whenever I was at the cashier finishing my shopping and some spent more time than usual helping me look curious at the female articles I was buying.

I started dressing again but had not been able to dress fully and felt incomplete. For me, it was not enough to wear only panties, hose, or any single piece of female clothing under my male clothes. I wanted and needed to see myself as a girl. How could I get married to a woman if I was feeling like that?

Reading the stories of crossdressers, transgenders, and transsexuals was an incredible source of knowledge and inspiration. I found many transsexuals that were well known by then and I wanted that for me so bad. But I was about to get married. How should I tell Maggie? Or should I keep my secret? Or should I tell her I don't want to get married without giving her the real reason? I felt confused. I tried to postpone our decision of setting a date to get married and it worked for a while.

We had some conversations about transsexuals. I already knew she didn't like anything related to the LGBT community but was not sure how deep her thoughts were about that. I found she was clearly not going to be supportive, so I decided to not open myself to her. I felt trapped again as when I was a child and a teenager. I loved her but I didn't dare to come out to her. I felt confused again. Was my mind playing games on me? Was it just a temporary phase again? Was it something I could get rid of so I can live the life many other "normal" men live? Those were my thoughts at that time.

Months before my marriage I remembered Eva, my ex-girlfriend who said I was hiding something. Now I understood what she meant. I was hiding my confusion from everyone, and my confusion was hiding a truth I was too afraid to accept or too blind to recognize. When in fear, you can run away or you can try covering yourself to avoid being hurt. It's like acting by survival instinct. Or you can get conscious of what is at stake and realize that fighting against the root of your fear might be the only way to set you free from it. I guess it all depends on your level of awareness about who you are and what you want. I can say building that level of awareness was something I didn't do at that time maybe because of being "distracted" with my coverings as Eva said to me. Looking back it is always easier to point out if what we decided was right or wrong. But we are analyzing based on the results we already know we have. I broke up with Maggie, and later we got back together. In the meantime, my insecurities were growing, and I asked her if I could take the time I needed for myself and we broke up again.

Being still alone gave me a chance to continue exploring myself. I remembered there was a movie titled "Ma Vie en Rose" that I was curious about. It was launched some years ago, but I couldn't watch it and it was not played in theatres anymore. When I remembered the movie, I searched for it on the Internet and found its synopsis and pictures of it. It was not the time of YouTube so I had no chance to find videos of it. I felt identified with that movie and whenever I was renting movies at video stores I was looking for it without success.

One day I was at a Blockbuster store searching for movies to watch alone at home and found "Ma Vie en Rose" was available for rent. I read the synopsis again. It was so familiar, so related to how I felt when I was a child. The main character, Ludovic, was a child who dreamed that one they he was going to be a girl. It was exactly as it happened to me! He thought it was just a matter of time before he would grow up and become a girl and he doesn't understand why his parents were so worried about him. Many of the scenes reminded me of my childhood, although the big difference was I never told anybody about I wanted to be a girl, but Ludovic did. All the consequences he faced, all the suffering, the pain, the fears, the frustration, were too much and I couldn't avoid crying and thinking that could have happened to me too. Why does society have to be like that? What's wrong if a person feels he or she wants to express in a given gender? What's the problem with that? Ludovic tried suicide, and that is a decision taken by many transgender people or people that don't conform to society's standards, because of feeling hopeless and outcasted. It is very sad.

I watched "Ma Vie en Rose" at least three times on a weekend. Each time I felt touched by it deeply and cried. I don't want to live a life in which I have to hide who I am. What can I do? Who can help me to solve my struggles? Ludovic found a girl that wanted to be a boy and only when that happened, the families realized all they needed was acceptance and love. I wished so much I could meet someone that can support me and help me to open myself as a girl to the world, and that was a hope I had alive since then.

71

I was alone again, crossdressing from time to time. There were beautiful girls at the office I was working, and I felt attracted to some of them, but for me, it was always more wishing I could be like them than willing to be in a loving relationship.

When my friends at work noticed I was spending time with a beautiful girl, but I was not doing anything to move forward with her, they couldn't understand what was happening to me. "Don't you like her? She likes you! Come on!", "She will think that you are gay", were the things they told me plus some jokes about that too. Besides Eva and Maggie, I can't remember other girls I fell in love with and had a loving relationship with. At that age, I didn't find myself attracted to men but maybe it was because of trying to build a standard masculine image of myself to feel more secure and to fit into society. I don't know.

Whenever someone was joking or saying that I had no girlfriend because I liked boys, I was getting angry but that only caused them to play more jokes about it. I decided to not pay attention to those comments and started to laugh at their jokes and played their game sometimes, but I started to seriously wonder if I could really be gay. I haven't considered being in love with a man but now I was wondering, because when dressed as a girl I had already felt that. I liked to dress as a girl very much, I wanted to be one of them but there were times I didn't want any part of that and wanted to know how to quit crossdressing forever and stop all my confusion. No matter how much I tried to not dress as a girl I was always going back to do it again.

Many times, when I was dressing as a girl, it happened that I started to have spontaneous thoughts about how it could be to be with a man as a girl. I tried to deny it but as I was dressing more and more those thoughts were increasing and I let them be. I noticed those thoughts were not happening when I was not dressed as a girl. It was strange and it was adding more confusion. Those were tough days with very difficult emotions and feelings to handle. I started dating girls again and maybe forcing me to act the standard male role contributed to feeling balanced for a while. That was when I met a girl named Gabriela at a party.

Gabriela was nice and pretty but I was not thinking of something else with her. However, she seemed interested and was flirting with me. She asked what my job was, and I decided to play a joke. "I am a makeup artist", I answered. She opened her eyes wide and said that was not possible. I asked why she said that and it was funny to look at her trying to find the right words to express her thoughts: "Because you don't look like one. I mean, I know not all makeup artists have to look or act feminine or be gay but...", she said still surprised and disappointed, I could tell. The conversation went into opinions about different gender expressions and sexuality and I realized it was going beyond where I wanted to play my joke. I thought it was the moment to tell her I was joking but she continued: "So, do you practice makeup on yourself? Because I know many makeup artists do that", she said. I was taken by surprise and didn't answer. "You do!", she exclaimed assuming my silence was an affirmation. I was about to say I was just joking but she asked: "Do you also dress like a girl sometimes?", she asked with the smile of who is expecting an affirmative answer. "No. I was just joking", I said and regretted having started the joke. I could have said whatever about my job, but I don't know why I said makeup artist. "Joking? Then why are you blushing?", she said. "It was only a joke, really", I insisted, and we changed the topic after that. It was the first and last time I saw her. The conversation left me wondering about my gender identity and sexuality once more.

Shopping for and buying women's clothes, lingerie, shoes, and makeup in person was something that challenged me a lot. At that time I was not able to buy online so there was no other way. Most of the time I was very nervous. I used to go to big stores in which I could walk around the female clothing section without having to talk to any attendant, just picking what I wanted and going directly to the cashier. There were always some women around and although I was thinking their eyes were all over me when I was staring at dresses, skirts, tops, lingerie and eventually picking an article, I learned with time that they were really into their own search for clothes and not caring at all about me. I believe it is all a matter of confidence and I must admit I was not confident at all and was scared to be pointed out. My mind was playing hard with myself every time I felt someone could discover I liked to dress as a female. Sometimes I pretended I was talking on my mobile phone, or checking a shopping list on paper, playing the act of having been sent to buy stuff for my girlfriend or wife. I changed my behavior as I was gaining more confidence when buying and walked freely around the women's section picking the stuff I wanted. My confidence never grew that much to try the clothes on at the store, but I learned very well how to check my size on female clothing.

After the times when I went through purges and threw away all my female stuff, the next time when going to shop for female stuff I was always very excited. Those days it was difficult for me to not want to buy all the beautiful dresses, lingerie, skirts, everything! I ended with a "too large" collection of clothes and makeup articles, including false nails and eyelashes, at the cashier. I didn't think about anything and just had a lot of fun choosing what I wanted without second thoughts, but in the waiting line I realized it was too evident that I couldn't be buying so much for someone else.

A couple of young girls I saw when I picked up my lingerie were just behind me in line. They looked at me and my shopping cart and I noticed they said something quietly. I was sure they were talking about me. I didn't know them but felt nervous. When it was my turn at the cashier a young lady greeted me and started to take all my articles out of the shopping cart. She was a very talkative person and I wanted to act as naturally as I could, but it was difficult. She started making comments about the tops and skirts, how they match, their beautiful colors, etc. She had comments for everything! I wanted to disappear! It was taking forever to get out and I wanted to leave. The girls behind me were close and I could see the surprise on their faces at all the female stuff I was buying. I was almost sure they were about to say something as they clearly noticed I was feeling uncomfortable at their looks. When the cashier finished with the makeup, nails, and eyelashes she asked me: "How do you know exactly what makeup to buy for your wife? It matches perfectly! Did she give you a list or something like that? She must be someone experienced at makeup to be so specific about what she asked you to buy for her!" She sounded gentle, and friendly, and did not like trying to expose me. She was not being ironic. I just smiled in silence, and she smiled back giving me a tender look. It was obvious to me that she knew all

74

that I had bought was for me and not for a girlfriend or wife. Maybe she just wanted to show me she was "on my side" trying to support me after noticing the behavior of the two young girls.

One day I was looking for another job and was searching for other alternatives not related to my profession. I was wondering if it was the time to explore something different and new in which I could work too. I didn't arrive at any conclusion on what new I could do until my mother told me she had a friend whose daughter was about my age that was making money appearing in some commercials on TV. She said the payment was per commercial filmed, but the money could be a lot for spending a couple of hours filming. To be considered for those commercials the candidates have to attend auditions first, and then have a photograph session to build a book that was going to be used by the marketing company to present the candidates to their potential customers of commercials for casting. I told my mother I was not interested, and I considered that going to auditions, photograph sessions, and castings was not something I was willing to do.

I remembered when I dreamed about being a supermodel when I was younger. I couldn't understand why I was not willing to do what candidates to models are supposed to do when they start so they can be known and then selected for a job. Today I think what was happening to me those days was that presenting myself to an audition or casting was related to becoming a male model, and I didn't want that. I wanted to be a female model, but that was something I was considering impossible.

One Saturday afternoon my mother called me and said she got a contact for me. It was her old friend, the one that convinced me when I was a kid to take part in a fashion show. That lady was still working in the fashion industry and had contacts in model scouting companies that make auditions for models in TV commercials. She said she was waiting for me to meet her so she can help me to get an audition. I told my mother to tell her friend I was not interested.

When I got home, I thought about the opportunity my mother was giving me with her friend and I played the game of attending and audition to be a model. By that time, I had already bought enough female clothes to have fun changing outfits and different looks pretending I was attending a casting and I was posing for photographers. I had fashion magazines with me, and I tried to strike the poses of the models that were there imitating them. Would anybody accept a woman that was born with a male body to be a female model? My answer was discouraging. Feeling hopeless, I cleaned my makeup, wore my male clothes, and went out for a walk.

I was walking alone in the street with no particular purpose than just to get some fresh air. There were people around and I was moving without thinking about a place where I wanted to go. The street was crowded as usual on a Saturday afternoon. I was standing in a corner waiting for the red light to change so I could cross the street. When the light changed and I was crossing the street to reach the other sidewalk, a young woman who was walking in the opposite direction stopped me politely and asked if she can talk to me. I was surprised but as she didn't look dangerous or suspicious, I accepted. We were in the middle of the street with a lot of people around, so I was sure nothing bad could happen.

The young woman introduced herself to me saying she was a model scout. She gave me her business card in which I could see her name, the name of the company she was working for, and her contact information. She was very extroverted, and I liked the way she approached me. Then she asked me if I was interested in filming a commercial for TV. Thinking giving it a second thought I answered I was not interested. The young woman insisted.

- Look, it's a good opportunity. I haven't seen you before but when I saw you crossing the street, I knew you are the perfect person for the commercial we have to film. – she said.

Her words sound to me as if she could be telling that to any other person and not only me, so I denied and tried to give her back her business card. She didn't give up.

- Yes, I know it looks and sounds weird and you may think I am lying or playing a joke. Please, keep my business card. You have nothing to lose. You can call the company and will find that it is real, the same as I am, and what I am saying is true. If you go there tomorrow at eleven o'clock in the morning, I will present you to the casting team and you will be selected for the commercial at once. I am sure. We need a man of your profile and the scene we need you to film is very simple. You just need to walk holding hands with a girl on the beach, make it look like you are in love, and then run after her when she attempts to go away from you. She has the main role. The commercial is for a well-known women's perfume brand. We need to film that scene tomorrow and we were about to postpone it because the other man had to decline as he had an emergency to attend to this weekend. If you accept now, I will contact the team to confirm we can film tomorrow. Of course, you will be paid, and I can assure you it will be a good amount of money for just a couple of hours on a Sunday. What do you say? – she said and it was too much to think she was lying. I still didn't like the idea of taking part in something like that. Thinking about the possibility of getting some unexpected cash, I forgot about my resistance to model as a male and end up accepting.

- Ok. I'll be there at 11 o'clock. – I said.

- That's awesome! Thank you! By the way, I am Catherine, but you have already seen my name on my business card. – she said and then asked my name and my telephone number just in case it was needed.

On Sunday morning I was telling myself how I could have been so foolish to believe what Catherine told me. It was true I had nothing to lose but I didn't feel like filming a commercial for TV. When I left home to go to the given address, I had no expectations at all and was sure everything was a lie and I was caught by a talkative extroverted girl that should be laughing about me. I was wrong.

When I arrived at the place, I saw the name of the company, and many people there, including filming equipment and staff moving around preparing to get into a van. Catherine was among them. She recognized me and was very happy to see I finally trusted her. She introduced me to the casting team. I felt uneasy and out of place. They noticed that and made me feel comfortable. They introduce me to Daniela, the girl who had the leading role in the commercial, with whom I was going to be in the scene I had to film. She was so pretty and was very nice too. I thought I could recognize her from other commercials I had seen before and she confirmed that. She was very experienced in filming while I had none.

- Don't worry! I'll help you! It will be fun! – Daniela said.

There were several scenes to be filmed at the beach. Mine was very short, no more than ten seconds when I watched the commercial on TV, but we filmed our scene for an hour, just because the production team wanted us to repeat the scene many times so they can film it from different angles and

77

asking us to try different movements and gestures. I enjoyed working with Daniela a lot, she made it very easy for me.

- Is there any scene when we should kiss? – she asked once. I knew that was not something we were supposed to do in our scene.

- No, Daniela. No kiss in this commercial. – said Catherine.

- That's a pity. I wouldn't mind kissing Eric, just so you know. – Daniela said flirting with me.

- You see, Dani? I told you, right? – I heard Catherine answering Daniela. Later Catherine told me Daniela was a lesbian.

Probably I would have felt uncomfortable with their jokes and comments if they were other people and in a different environment. Maybe they really found me attractive or were just having fun with me. That didn't matter to me. I have to say I liked the experience of filming with such a beautiful, experienced and professional girl and also a very professional staff. I was very well paid too. That made me think modeling could be a source of income for me, even though I was reluctant to accept I should have to do it as a male.

Catherine called me many times after that for other commercials. I accepted to film a couple more until I felt I didn't want to do it any longer. Without a real intention, I was starting to project to the public an image of a man that I didn't want to. Today I think I could have given myself more chances on that. Who knows. Maybe that could have opened other doors to meet different people in an artistic environment where usually people are more open-minded.

78

I built a large wardrobe of female clothes while living alone, but after some time I went through another purge after another episode of stress because of my gender identity and sexuality issues. It was like I was in a fight against myself and everything around me. I needed to find balance and thought that a new purge could help me.

I worked hard on building my balance acting the male role as much as I could. After some time, Maggie and I got back together once more and soon after that, we set up the date of our marriage. I loved her so much and she loved me too. We were a "perfect couple", as our friends and relatives said, and all of them were happy that we were together again and going to get married.

A day before I got married, I had to be sure to get rid of any remaining female stuff I had to avoid any chance of having them been found by Maggie once she moved in with me. It was not difficult because I had already decided I was not going to crossdress again and I had already purged a large collection of female clothes before. I was, again, trying to convince myself that if I was not crossdressing anymore my desires would reduce until they would eventually disappear. It was a reasoning like the more time I could stay away from that the sooner I was going to be able to overcome it. Not having any female article of my own was key to supporting that reasoning, and I also thought that having Maggie living with me was going to help me focus on our life together and sooner or later I was going to leave behind all my gender identity and sexuality issues from my past.

Married life came full of new things and experiences and that helped a lot to have a different mindset with new life goals. All that contributed to setting my issues aside and I didn't think again about that for years.

As in the previous stages of my life, sooner or later something was going to trigger my compulsion to dress again. Repressing something without really working on understanding what is happening at its core only adds more to a pressure cooker effect until it can't be contained anymore. But I had thought I could.

Maggie and I were having a happy relationship and were living a happy family life. We had our first child and then a second one and had to move to a bigger apartment. After we finished moving, there were many things we left in the previous apartment that I had to throw away. While doing that I found a package of old clothes that Maggie had left to throw away. There was a red mini dress I didn't remember seeing her wear before. I held it for a while. Being alone in that place with plenty of time and having found that dress was, again, a big temptation. It reminded me of the moment I had when moving from my old house after finishing university. It was the same situation. It was like my life was exposing me to situations where I was not able to think about my promise of not dressing again and I had to move on based on my desires. Was it like an addiction that was out of control? I hadn't crossdressed or thought about crossdressing for years, but I felt I had to wear that red mini dress. I felt a rush running all over my body and

79

hitting my mind opening the old locked door of my gender issues once more. "Why am I doing this again?", I asked myself when I was putting the red mini dress on, and the answer was a silent smile. It felt so right, so comfortable, so "this is me".

I was crossdressing again after many years no matter how much I tried not to. I looked at myself in the mirror and something was not right. I had kept my hair short for years. I had forgotten when I used to have it long to my shoulders at least and that was enough to achieve a female look at that time whenever I crossdressed when I was younger. I had to grow my hair again, but it would take too long so I thought I could use a wig to achieve a better look. I went back home but taking the red mini dress in a bag. I found a place to hide it in the new apartment. My mind was running wild at the idea of getting a wig and that same night I was on the Internet browsing online shopping websites where I could get a female wig. My heart was pounding hard when I completed my purchase. It was a long dark chocolate brown wig. I was careful to have it sent to my mother's address to avoid the risk of getting it at home.

Days later, when I finally got my wig, I was thrilled at the idea of trying it, but my mind wanted to go further. My "inner girl" was woken up again and stronger than ever before. I ended entering a shoe store and bought my first own high heels. I felt uncomfortable when I entered the store and had not even planned what to say to the attendant in case I was asked. It was natural when the young girl approached me when I was staring at a pair of beautiful high heels and she asked if I needed help and I said I wanted to buy those and gave her a shoe size. I didn't have to say they were not for me. She brought them and then I paid and went out. I was surprised at how easy it had been and was encouraged for more. I was driven by my female desires and it felt so good. I went to a makeup store and entered without second thoughts and asked a lady for help to prepare a package of makeup for a "gift". She was very friendly and only asked me "What type of skin she has?". I answered immediately that it was like mine. She took me to a desk and started showing me lipsticks, eyeshadow, foundation, mascara, blush, eyeliner, and other stuff I didn't know. She said, "If she has your skin and your green eyes, she will look gorgeous with these", and she prepared a makeup set with all of what she showed me. I can't explain how I felt when I left the store. The incredible feeling of imagining myself completely dolled up was back and had grown its intensity. Finding time to crossdress at home with my wife and children was almost impossible and that caused anxiety, but finally it happened.

One day I had to work overnight and had the next day off. With my wife at work and my children at school and nursery, I had the time alone I was looking for and it was amazing. When I finished my makeup and wore the red mini dress and heels and put my wig on and looked at the mirror, I almost couldn't believe it was me. I had never dressed that way with makeup and a gorgeous wig. I was amazed at my female image and what I was feeling. Every time I worked overnight, I knew I was going to enjoy my time alone to dress the next day and wanted to have different clothes to try and to practice my makeup again. I became addicted to overnight work looking forward to the chance of being at home fully dressed the next day. What would happen if my wife came home earlier? What would happen if I was called to pick up my children from school or nursery? I ask these questions now, but I was not asking them back then. I needed to have my time and the rest was left aside and not considered as something that could happen. It was a bit of a scary attitude because I was not anymore that kid who was sneaking into his sister's and mother's drawers risking being caught.

As time was passing, I was building again a large collection of female stuff I could keep safe from being discovered. One day I was with Maggie walking on the street and she met a girlfriend. She was a very attractive brunette with green eyes. It was impossible not to look at her and the red mini-dress she was wearing was exactly like the one I had at home! I loved her look, her makeup, the way she walked, talked, moved, her smile, the way she touched her long dark chocolate brown hair..., just like the wig I had. Maggie introduced us and said to me: "Honey, let me introduce Karen, a former workmate". Back home in my next chance to dress fully I wore that red mini dress again and looked at myself in the mirror. "Nice to meet you, Karen," I said to myself and decided to adopt that name for me from that moment on.

Having a female name of my own generated a good feeling about myself. I had a female name and I had a female image that I could address with a proper name and that made me happy. Years later I added "Lyra" as my surname. It came after I found something named "frequency paintings". They were paintings that seemed to be like very colorful and beautiful stained glass. When I read some of their meanings or what was behind the purpose of the painting itself, I got caught by the painting named "Lyra" and its meaning. For me, it was describing clearly what I was feeling in my "finding myself" research. From that day on I became "Karen Lyra".

After I chose my female name, I was feeling more comfortable every time I was dressed. I continued buying clothes and some jewelry too. I bought some clip-on earrings but was willing to try some for which I needed to pierce my ears again. I remembered the first time I did that, so long ago, and what I heard about the little hole in my earlobe would close by itself in a few days if I didn't use earrings all the time. It happened that way and I wanted to try again. I had the chance on a business trip that would last longer than usual and the first night at the hotel I pierced my ears again.

When I dressed that night and was able to use the new earrings, I was so happy. I took good care of my pierced ears to avoid infections and everything went well. The day after nobody at work noticed my ears were pierced or they didn't say anything if they noticed. Back home they were not noticeable.

During that business trip, I took a digital camera and it was my first time taking pictures of me as a woman. It was great fun to be modeling different outfits even if only in private and taking pictures. I built a profile on a website to share my photos and chat with other girls like me and learn from them. To complete my profile, I had to choose if I was a crossdresser, transgender, transsexual, etc. I realized I didn't know enough about all those definitions and didn't know if I fit in any. I searched and learned as much as I could, but it seemed to me there were way too many labels, and the difference of some definitions was not always clear to me. Anyway, it helped me to find out how I was feeling. I was not dressing in female clothes because of sexual excitement. I was not dressing in female clothes because it gave me some relaxation and eased the stress. I thought about it consciously and was working on understanding myself as I should have done many years ago. I was dressing in female clothes because I understood I was a woman on the inside and making my external look match my inner image was what I was looking for. That was

81

my conclusion. What does that make me? I had deep thoughts about considering that there was more to it than just dressing in female clothes. I wanted to have changes in my body to make it feminine and wanted to live as a woman. I know in the past I had thought I wanted to be a girl but being an adult with a family and still thinking about that made it different. I wanted to think about the steps I should follow to achieve transition, become a woman, and live full-time as one. Immediately after thinking deeply about all that I felt discouraged. It was not going to be easy at all, I already knew that, but it took a different dimension considering it seriously as my life path. I was scared, I admit. I was scared at how I was going to follow that path that would end in making my life match my soul, which was my ultimate desire while causing pain and hurting my loved ones in the process as I was sure none of them, my wife included, were going to be supportive. It was a decision I was not ready to take and felt frustrated and depressed when thinking that following my wish meant breaking with my family. I felt sad during that time and didn't dress in female clothes even if having a chance.

At a family gathering the topic of transgender people was spontaneously discussed. My sadness became deeper when I confirmed the position of my wife and my relatives. I was the only one who expressed a point of view in favor of transgender people. I realized their radical position based on religious reasons or just "simple common sense" or "normal behavior" as they called it would not be changed. They were not disrespectful but closed-minded to me. At home, I tried to explain to Maggie about my perspective, but she was not willing to listen. I insisted but it was in vain. The next day I found myself alone at home but didn't dress as a female. I was upset and discouraged. My gender issues were causing stress again. I knew what I wanted but felt alone and hopeless. Angry, I put all my female stuff in a couple of bags and threw them away. Later I regretted my decision, but it was over. I couldn't dress again and got more depressed. I realized I was punishing the girl in me. It was not fair. She was not my "inner girl". She was me; I was her; we were one. We had been one for all my life and I had to reach acceptance about that. I knew it was going to take a while but sooner or later my need to express my female desires would be so intense again that I would not be able to repress them anymore. I had understood the lessons, but maybe not learned them well. One year later something different happened.

I was not feeling compelled to dress as a woman but getting deeply depressed and wanted to find help. After long research, finally, I found a gender therapist and had my first session. It was an online session. To prepare for it I had to complete a written template and for the first time in my life after so many years of struggling with my gender issues, I was putting in writing my experiences and feelings about it. It was a very helpful exercise. Talking openly with the therapist was strange at the beginning. She was addressing me as Karen, referring to me as a woman. I had never talked to anybody like that before, face to face, although it was a video conference. I felt better soon and after a few minutes, I was comfortable sharing my thoughts, explaining my feelings, and listening to her guiding questions, comments, and advice. She asked me why I was not presenting myself to her with a female image. I answered I had no female stuff at that time due to my last purge. She said it would help me if next time I presented myself as Karen, the woman I am.

Two weeks later I went out on a business trip and managed to buy a wig, some makeup, and a dress. When I was preparing for my next gender therapy session, I found myself in front of the mirror doing my makeup excited at the idea of being seen for the first time as Karen by another person. I was so nervous and anxious at the same time. When we started the session, I could feel my heart jumping off my chest in anticipation until the therapist appeared on the screen and said: "Hi Karen! I am so glad to see you!" The session was awesome. After it finished, I stayed in my hotel room for the rest of the night studying the information she gave me and writing a summary of the session preparing a plan of things to do for the next session until I fell asleep completely dressed and slept relaxed and happy like it had not happened for so long.

After my first two gender therapy sessions I was feeling motivated. I still had no idea of how I was going to move forward with transition but at least I stopped the negative thinking that was depressing me before. "Baby steps", the gender therapist told me suggesting I should look at easy and short-term achievable goals and don't rush in the process. Everyone has their own pace to do things and for transition, it is the same. There is no unique program or list of tasks to follow that can help everyone that wants to transition. I imagine there are some common guidelines, but everyone is different and needs to work on their own path.

The therapist guided me in a way I liked. She explained to me about gender dysphoria and told me she will guide me on the process, but transition is more a self-discovery journey than anything else. She recommended me write a diary with all that I was learning, discovering, planning, and achieving; to write down things I considered to be part of my process and try to do something about it. One thing, in my case, was to find someone I can fully trust that I believe could be open to understanding me and supporting me in the future with my transition. I didn't need to talk to that person right away but after identifying him or her I should write a coming out letter. The exercise of thinking about who that person could be was very interesting. I needed an ally. Who could it be? I wrote a list and went across several of my friends, and I ended with two I was almost sure could be the person I needed. I decided I was going to come out to one of them, Eva, my first girlfriend with whom I was very close in the past. I wrote her a letter. Writing that letter was a special and helpful experience. After I finished it, I was fully convinced she was going to be supportive, and I tried to find a way to get in contact with her again to meet soon and come out to her as transgender. The idea of these exercises was not to push me to take action unless I felt ready, but they were very motivating indeed. "Confidence is built by winning battles, no matter how little they may seem. Sooner or later those little wins will be adding to your confidence, and you will feel ready to take another step". Those words from the gender therapist made a lot of sense to me and based on them I took my baby steps one by one. After thinking and planning I decided my next step was to go out in public dressed as a woman. The idea was giving me goosebumps, but I needed to have that experience. I wanted it, prepared for it, and it happened.

The first time I went out in public dressed as a woman was a wonderful experience. I was abroad and staying at an apartment was better for my planned first time going out. At hotels, it is necessary to pass by the reception and lobby where there is always someone around no matter the time. At that apartment where I stayed, it was easier to go out and get back in without crossing with someone I could have met before. At least the chance was less.

Once on the street it was simply amazing. Used to be always indoors when dressed as a woman, being outside and feeling my heels on the sidewalk, the air on my face, my skirt being slightly moved by the wind, my heart slowing down getting used to the moment, was an incredible experience. It was early at night. I passed by some people on my way to a park nearby, but they didn't seem to care about me. If they did, I didn't notice. Sitting on a bench at the park and looking at a few people walking close without second looks at me was something I was not expecting. I was afraid of the idea of meeting people that could discover I was transgender and how they would react. Building confidence takes time and that first time out, even though I was alone and didn't talk to anybody, was a great first step for me. I went out dressed as a woman a couple more times while staying at that place. That week was full of experiences, including a completely not expected encounter with a man that left me deeply affected.

On the last night of that business trip, I decided to go out as a woman again. It was a bit later than the previous nights and there were fewer people around. I walked through a park, crossed a bridge and when I was there just looking at the city landscape and its lights under the stars and the moon, a man appeared out of nowhere. Maybe he was following me, and I didn't notice. He didn't look aggressive, but I felt uncomfortable with his presence. He spoke to me and I pretended I didn't understand what he said and tried to leave walking back to the bridge. He held one of my arms firmly and said he was not going to let me go anywhere. His words frightened me and I wanted to run away. He looked athletic and was stronger than me. I knew it was going to be very hard to fight him or try to run. He pulled me towards his body and forced his arms around me pressing my body against him. Surprised and scared I thought that if I showed him I wanted to go, he would try to force me violently and I thought it was better to avoid that. Acting the way he was, appearing out of nowhere, I wondered if he had a gun or a knife to threaten me. My survival instinct told me not to fight, at least not at that moment. When he realized I was not trying to leave, he released me and asked me to have sex with him. A long time ago, when I was a teenager, I had fantasized about being with a man when I was dressing as a woman, it had passed so many years ago and I had never thought about that anymore. I didn't answer his request, so he insisted and pulled me against him again telling me he was not going to hurt me if I was going to do as he wanted. He tried to kiss me on my lips once and I moved my head away, so he took my head strongly and forced me to let him kiss my lips. He stopped kissing me and insisted he wanted to have sex with me right there. I tried to push him back when he was surrounding my body tightly with his strong arms and knew then that fighting him was not going to work. He was very strong. There was nobody around to cry for help and I thought that I could escape if I showed him I was not going to fight. He kissed me again and I kissed him back without thinking much about the kiss itself. He calmed down a bit. My mind was running wild trying to find a way to escape without making him feel like I didn't want to stay. He released me saying I shouldn't try to leave or he was going to use something against me and put one of his hands into a pocket of his jacket like about to bring out a weapon. I couldn't tell if it was a gun but, for me, he had something there and I didn't want him to take it out. He asked me to walk a couple of steps behind some bushes and I obeyed begging to find somebody that could help me. He held me again firmly and said he wanted to have sex with me right there and if I was a good girl he was not going to hurt me. This time it was me who kissed him on his lips to make him feel I was not going away. He seemed to calm down and I thought about something I could do to gain time and find a way out. I put my hand on his lap and felt his hard penis. He liked when I did that and he immediately unzipped his pants and I helped to pull them down while he was still holding one

84

of my arms very firmly and strong to not let me go. I put myself on my knees in front of him, saw his big hard penis in front of me, I closed my eyes and got it into my mouth. He pushed his penis into my mouth and moved his hips forward while he was moving my head to get his pleasure. I haven't ever imagined giving oral sex to a stranger. I was doing it, but my mind was on another thing and not on his penis or what I was feeling in my mouth. I continued giving him oral sex and he released my arm and my head as he was moaning and about to ejaculate inside my mouth. He took his jacket out and let it fall. I knew that was the moment I needed and so I moved apart, took his jacket with me, and ran as fast as I could to cross the bridge to where I could find help. He was shouting at me and he was trying his pants back on with some difficulty and started to run after me. But I had gained some distance and time, even though I was running in high heels. I reached the other side of the bridge and checked his jacket. There was no gun in it. I threw the jacket down a stairway of the bridge and kept on running. Maybe he tried to recover his jacket instead of chasing me. I don't know. After a couple of blocks, I found some people walking around and I felt safe. I was lucky to have lost him. Maybe that was the most frightening moment of all my life. I was between a storm of thoughts and reproving myself for all that had happened. Why did I cross that bridge alone late that night? I was shouting to myself that I had been very stupid to go out that way. I could have been raped or even killed, and I had to admit I had to be grateful for having had the chance to escape, even if that meant to have given oral sex to a man, a stranger to me, in the street.

I got back to the building and when I was fully sure that man was not near and couldn't see me, I entered the building and felt completely safe. Confused, afraid, surprised, but safe. The visions of what happened with that man were repeating constantly in my mind like forcing me to remember everything, every detail, every emotion, and feeling. It was overwhelming. That same night I also met an old lady inside the building after getting back, just when I was about to open the door of my apartment, still trembling from the terrible experience. She lived next door on the same floor and we had met days before on the corridor, being me as a male. She was very friendly and we knew our first names from the very first day we met. That night, when she suddenly appeared and looked at me all dressed up as a woman and about to open my door nervously, she greeted saying my male name and I dropped my keys to the floor. I had no doubt she had recognized me. I felt like dying and I didn't want to look at her and wanted to vanish right there. She greeted me again with her friendly voice. I looked back at her very nervous without saying a word and trying to smile. "Take it easy, young lady. You'll be all right.", she said to me with a tender voice and friendly smile and then continued her way.

That night, my mind was recreating all the situations with that stranger. I couldn't believe what had happened, what I did. I shouldn't have gone out that way, so restless. Although I was feeling afraid and traumatized, I knew I had been lucky. It could have been worse if that man could have been armed. I decided I was never going out by myself at night to places with few people.

After that experience, my issues were not anymore about my gender identity but my sexuality too. As it had happened when I was a teenager, I started to think about being with a man, sexually, whenever I was dressing as a woman, and only when dressing as a woman. I

85

couldn't think of myself as a man being with another man, but whenever I was looking at myself as a girl, I was noticing how my desire to be treated like one by a man was strongly revealing.

I didn't share the experience with my gender therapist. I believe it would have been better, but I had mixed emotions about what had happened and preferred to process it all better before sharing it. I did mention that I was thinking about men when I was dressing as a woman. She asked me if I liked men and I think it was hard for me to say "yes" because I had been fighting all my life with not accepting I could be gay. I said, "I am not sure", and explained that I had thought about it but only while being dressed as a woman. She said it was ok to not be sure, it was ok to not know because I was just starting to build my awareness as a woman and so my feelings were mixed with my beliefs, cultural and religious, and my entire life experience as a man. She suggested that I take it easy because sooner or later all my deep feelings would come out as they should, openly and sincerely.

After two more gender therapy sessions the therapist told me it could be very helpful if I started trying androgen blockers to lower my testosterone levels before planning my transition. That could help me cope with gender dysphoria when I was not able to dress as a woman. She wrote me a letter in which she described my case of gender dysphoria and recommended to follow hormone replacement therapy. When I read at the top of the letter "Miss Karen Lyra, former Eric Robins…" it was surreal. Was that really happening? I haven't solved the puzzle of my family and job situation yet but already had the green light to start hormones! I could not believe that was happening. I was standing at the door I was dreaming of opening for so long, but I hadn't come out to anybody, not in my family, not in my job. How was I going to start transition with permanent changes in my body's appearance without telling my wife, children, family, and co-workers? I knew I was not going to get any support from my family and relatives, they were completely against transgender people. The same happened in my job so I was going to need another one. From what I knew, it was going to be far too complicated to get a well-paying job to support my family and my transition. Every decision we make in life has a price that we have to pay. It is a difficult puzzle to solve. I needed to plan, to meditate very carefully on how I was going to move from here to there. I was looking for a sign, something that could help me make the decision that was going to change my life forever.

I am the kind of person that thinks everything happens for a reason that I may not understand at the moment it happens, so I need to stay alert to reach a deep understanding of the event. I used to say it was something good or bad. Now I think it is an experience from which I can decide whether to grow or not even if I didn't like it.

Having the chance to start hormones to begin my transition was something I was looking forward to for years, consciously or not, since the moment I knew the story of Caroline Cossey. When I finally reached that point, I realized I had not experienced real life as a woman at all. I was about to start hormones but was not yet out to anyone. I had yet to meet Eva, the ex-girlfriend to whom I wrote my coming out letter. She had traveled abroad, and I felt I should tell her personally and not by email. My gender therapist told me I didn't need to decide to go fully into hormone therapy but that I could try anti-androgens first only for a couple of months. Taking them for that short time wouldn't cause any changes in my body that I should worry about but would lower my testosterone level which would help me with my gender dysphoria.

I felt it was a good idea and started with a couple of pills she recommended, Spironolactone and Finasteride. The first one was going to help lower my testosterone and the second one was going to help with the hair loss that I had started to develop. I was concerned about side effects after reading a lot about hormone replacement therapy (HRT). I remember at least six months of HRT was needed to have noticeable physical changes. As I was not going to try that longer then I felt it was safe doing it on my own while I was finding out how to solve my "family & job" puzzle.

I started taking the pills but I cannot remember something significant happening in terms of mood change or sex drive changes for those months that I took the pills. After two months of taking them, I thought I could try some estrogen patches and see what effects they could have on me. I was conscious, from all that I had read about HRT, that self-medication was dangerous and should be avoided. It was highly recommended to have this process under the control of an endocrinologist. I found one in my city that was treating some transgender people with whom I was chatting in a forum. I made an appointment with him and he asked me to take some blood tests in advance with specific details about the indicators he wanted to check. I tried taking those blood tests but was told they were not covered by my medical insurance. I didn't insist. I was worried that if I was about to take tests and follow up with an endocrinologist all that was going to be part of my medical records and that could be known by my wife or any relative time later. I didn't want that. I started applying estrogen patches by myself, committed to stopping at any sign of something going wrong with my health. It was not easy to hide the estrogen patch on my body from my wife, but I found a way. I was into the third month of taking the anti-androgens and now I was taking estrogen too. I didn't feel anything relevant by the end of the third month until I remember I started to feel fatigued like never before. I have been always a very active person, loving sports and practicing them a lot. The fatigue I was feeling was not like that of being tired after a hard training session. I was eating as usual, very healthy, and drinking water, I was not a smoker or a drinker at all and my overall health seemed good to me, but the sensation of fatigue increased day by day. I stopped the pills and the patches and went to the doctor. I didn't mention anything about the pills and patches. After some tests, the doctor told me something was wrong with my kidneys and there were too many toxins in my blood. I followed the indications of the doctor and after a month I was feeling better but not as before. I felt discouraged and very worried about my health. I left aside my ideas about coming out, transition plans, and dressing. I stopped everything related to that. I stopped the gender therapy sessions too. I was angry with myself as I was sure my health was badly affected by the pills and patches I used. Maybe all that happened to me were side effects that would go away with time. Or maybe it was just a pure coincidence and there was something wrong with my health that manifested at the moment I took the pills and used the patches. Maybe this is something I will never know.

After I recovered, I continued practicing sports as before but took it easy. Some months later I was taking a long flight back home after a business trip. I was already not feeling well during the trip that lasted one week. When I got back home, I had difficulty walking. The next day I went to the doctor again. My kidneys were failing. The condition was solved after almost three months of treatment. As a result of all this, I cannot take any type of medication from that moment on without close supervision unless it was urgent. It could trigger health issues again.

Why did all this happen? I knew I still had some key situations to solve before starting transition as I wanted but then it was clear to me that the path of transition was not available anymore, at least I couldn't see a way. I learned some transgender people live full-time as women without going through HRT, but I felt different. I wanted to have my body matching my soul completely and that was not going to be possible without HRT. Gender dysphoria hit harder than ever during those days leading to strong depression again. I went into another purge and threw away all my female stuff. This time it caused a lot of pain. It took me a long time to accept the situation.

The fact of discarding transition slowed down my female desires, I guess. I ended up not coming out to Eva and found no reason to do it with her or anybody else. I felt not compelled to dress as a woman anymore during that time. I removed my profiles on the social media sites where I was active as Karen. I felt I needed to forget about all that. It hurt, but I was angry with myself and, again, punishing myself one more time. I wondered why I had to live my life that way. I wondered what could happen so I could follow the path I wanted. I thought about myself when I was younger and how I wished I could have known more back then so I would definitively have taken other decisions... and I would be already living as a woman. Thinking about those things didn't help me at all and only added more sadness and stress.

Time heals everything, they say. And I guess in my case it was more than just the physical type of healing. I realized I haven't honestly and deeply accepted myself fully, with the inner boy and inner girl together because I am both. The "69" in my email and some social media accounts is not for a sexual connotation as some have thought. It is, for me, the Yin Yang, the complete balance of opposites that makes the beauty in life and what I have assumed as my goal for having a body that doesn't match my soul. With time, lots of reading, and more of writing, I felt comfortable with myself and my situation. I was not giving up my wishes but decided I was not going to push myself. I didn't know how things could happen for me to get where I want but that didn't bother me like it did before. I began feeling at peace with myself and was not angry anymore. After some time, I bought new dresses, wigs, shoes, makeup, lingerie, and body enhancements wearing articles to achieve the female image I want when I dress, and I keep doing it as much as I can while I also keep working out to have a healthy body I can feel happy with. I felt grateful for all that happened so far and focus on continuing getting chances to grow as a person more than anything else.

Today I think that maybe I was looking too much outside of myself, too much about the physical image I wanted to achieve, and I lost track of what was more important: to look inside me with complete honesty, compassion, and love. I needed to let myself love myself for who I am, not just look to what I wanted to become. Can a seed grow into a plant that can give beautiful flowers tomorrow without water? Can I grow as a human being without loving myself for who I am today?

Looking for a clue on how to feel better about myself I continued wondering what could have happened if I made other decisions related to being transgender when I was younger. That opened the door to daydreaming about how my life would be now and how happy it could be. However, some of those times also led me to think about how I did not decide differently and I found myself being hard on myself for those decisions I took, and I got into negative emotions about it. Looking at the past is necessary as we can learn from it but sometimes it could be harmful and unfair because I could be judging my younger self with the experience and knowledge I have today, even though there is still a lot that I need to experience and learn. Getting stuck there is useless as I can't change the past and that can be an auto-destructive behavior. I thought maybe I could work on those emotions to process them as needed, understand them, and let them go to free myself from the pain and sadness and get myself open for love. The last time I had that negative thinking happening again, I was aware enough to realize I was being hard on myself, so I decided to do something different to help me. If I am going to daydream about my past, instead of judging maybe I can imagine I can meet my younger self, my "inner girl" who is confused, sad, and afraid about what she is feeling as a transgender person. I know she is wondering what she could be in her life while she is feeling trapped, and helpless, and still had to take those decisions with the little she knew back then. I thought about it and if I could meet her, I would not judge her but would hug and comfort her. I would hold her in my arms lovingly and I am sure she would cry on my shoulder as if I were the shelter she couldn't find at those tough times so she can release her feelings and emotions finding some relief, finally. I would thank her for moving forward the way she did, with all the difficulties she had to face, and maybe at that moment I would find myself whispering a song to her:

"Caterpillar in the tree,

how you wonder who you'll be,

can't go far but you can always dream.

Wish you may and wish you might,

don't you worry hold on tight,

I promise you that there will come a day...

Butterfly fly away."

And maybe as I finish whispering, she falls asleep in my arms feeling safe, loved, and in peace as she always deserved.

My gender identity and sexuality issues are not gone but they have lost the relevance they had in my life from the moment I accepted myself. I have realized who I am and have decided to let me embrace that realization and find inner peace, finally, no matter if I have no idea if someday I will come out, transition, and live as a woman. I live as a human being that has learned to love who I am, every single part of my body and soul, mind, and heart, and has finally achieved finding my truth to be able to love others openly in the same way.

89

Part 2

I believe one of the most important things for any human being is to realize who they are, deep inside ourselves, and not just behave according to the societal standards (that change all the time) or the culture we live in (that also changes with time) or the education we were given by our parents, relatives, and school, or by the traditions and manners we inherited due to our family and the place we were born (religion, food, sports, etc.…). I am a strong believer that if we don't question ourselves deeply and honestly, trying to step back from what we are doing most of our time on "auto-pilot" mode, to give ourselves time to think why we are the way we are, why we behave the way we behave, why we feel what we feel, we might end up repeating patterns in our lives that our parents and ancestors repeated too, putting our genuine personality and human individual potential at risk. It is not an easy thing to do, especially when we find out we might need to swim upstream and face more difficulties in life than we would like to be ourselves.

It was difficult for me to find out whom I was given my own circumstances that I have shared in the first part of this book. I have read stories of others that have gone through really very dramatic and sometimes fatal circumstances to live the life they wanted for themselves, without hurting anybody, but they were hurt, and even killed. I am lucky and I am grateful. I am not yet in the group of the brave ones that raise their voice and speak up that they are transgender and live accordingly, taking big risks. I know I am still hiding in the dark, deep inside the closet and I will build my courage to come out one day. At this moment it is not my priority due to family reasons and that is why I remain anonymous but with the strong hope that maybe what I have shared in this book could help someone like me in his or her own gender identity discovery journey.

"How do I know if I am transgender?". I asked myself this question many times for years. I found answers to this question on the Internet from several male-to-female transgender people. Some of them had already gone through transition and surgery, living full-time as women while others were like me, not even out to some of their friends or family. Through the answers I read and the videos I watched I was trying to understand my own case. Before the Internet, I didn't know about the terms and definitions used for gender identity variances and their expressions. Trying to understand them was confusing but I also needed to realize how broad the gender identity spectrum was. In my case, I started thinking of myself as a crossdresser. The fact of liking so much to dress in female clothes while still identifying myself as a male made me think of it that way when I was young. I learned some males dressed as females because they like the clothes, they may experience sexual arousal while doing it or just want to express their feminine side but have no intention of moving forward with it in a way that could involve transforming their physical appearance using hormones or surgery and live as a woman one day. They felt like men with a strong desire of expressing a female side sometimes, some more often than others, but it seemed there were no issues related to how they perceived their gender. Also, others perceived themselves as female and were confused and stressed about the fact of having a male

91

body. My understanding at that moment was they were transgender. Maybe I sound too simplistic but that was the way I was thinking at that time with the information I could get.

I liked female clothes and I liked to express my feminine side but for me, it was clear that I wanted to be a girl since I was very young, and was puzzled at why I had to have the body of a boy. With time I learned my trouble and pain with my male physical features were the origin of what I understood as what is now called gender dysphoria. At that moment I learned that it was officially named as a disorder under what is called the DSM (Diagnosis and Statistical Manual of Mental Disorder Manual), a manual issued by the American Psychiatric Association that is updated as medical and scientific research and studies make progress on what are considered mental disorders and how to diagnose and treat them. I found that manual and read what it has to say about crossdressing, transvestites, transgender, etc. from a medical and professional point of view. My understanding back then was that I was having a sort of mental disorder that should be treated. Something was "wrong" with me. Years later I read in the latest version of that manual (DSM-5) there were many changes in what was related to gender identity and "Gender Dysphoria" was not considered a disorder anymore. I'm no expert in gender definitions and all that and don't rule my life by books that change with time, but I considered it important to try to understand what the professional approach is to what I was feeling, even if I disagreed. I arrived at the thought that I had issues with my gender identity and started to consider that maybe I was not a crossdresser. Maybe it was that crossdressing was becoming so intense that my awareness was starting to move from "I love to wear female clothes" to "I dress to make my inner self match my physical image". That was my case. That was the moment I felt I wanted to find professional guidance.

Among the girls that I followed on the Internet in those days during the mid-90s, I found a young crossdresser that caught my attention. I followed her for years amazed at her beauty and class, her feminine and fresh look. I wanted to dress and take pictures to build my own web page like her. I was so happy whenever she was sharing a new set of pictures with something about her. I remember reading from her early website updates that she considered herself a crossdresser with no intention of one day moving beyond that. Hormones and transition into a woman were not her plans at all, as she said. She was dressing more and more often and was looking prettier and more confident with time. She was an inspiration to me and, suddenly, she disappeared. Her site was brought down and I found later some websites in which there were some of her photos, but she was gone. There were comments that after so many years of crossdressing, she finally had changed her mind and decided she was going stealth to transition and live as a woman. She started as a crossdresser and never considered herself transgender at the beginning but later she did. What made her change her mind? I thought it was maybe because her desire grew more and more as she was dressing more often trying to look more feminine every time until she was not satisfied anymore. I am guessing. That was my understanding and at a given point in my life I did the same later. I wanted to know and understand myself more and tried to dress every time I could and found a way to manage dressing as a woman every other day for a year or two or for a complete week when traveling. Finally, I realized my desires had grown more and an intense feeling of disliking my male features became stronger as they were becoming difficult to hide when I tried to achieve a female image when dressing. That was how I realized I had strong gender dysphoria and concluded I am a male-to-female transgender. When I was able to get support and guidance from a gender therapist and I was told there was nothing "wrong" with me and I was transgender, it was a reaffirmation. However, the therapist said it was not because she was telling me that I was transgender that I should accept it. It was because I had discovered it is true after sincerely and deeply asking my heart through my experiences and research. "It's important that you get to this new awareness about your gender identity not because you are told but because you feel it. Once you get to this point it becomes a matter of planning how to move forward from there.", she said. That "moving from there" could mean many different things depending on each person. You may continue staying the way you are if you feel good like that or do something about it if you don't. It's where your journey can begin or not but is always something that should come from you. "Be always curious and search", said my grandmother many times when I was a kid, and I am still trying to keep that attitude in my life.

I love books, there is something interesting that happens when I grab one and look at its cover trying to imagine what I could find inside it before I read it. Once I read a book, sometimes I realize it was not what I expected, or it went far beyond where I thought it could take me and I feel amazed.

The cover and the title of a book can say a lot but that is what we see and it can be very different once we go deep into its pages. It is the same as when we see a person on the street and maybe we feel attracted to the image that is in front of us. Because we feel attracted to what we see outside doesn't mean we will continue to feel attracted once we have the chance to look at its inside by talking to that person face to face when we can and see how that person speaks, behaves, tells about its experiences, its mindset, body language..., and more. We could feel captivated by its personality and realize that could be the beginning of an interesting relationship. I believe that is exactly what happens with some books too.

In one of the books I read a while ago, which I have forgotten its title and author, there was a dialogue between a group of students and a teacher. They were discussing how different a story of a given book was compared to what its cover and title suggested. The dialogue was something like this: "We are like books too. People see how we look like and may even know our names and can imagine about us and our lives. Maybe they have even heard something about us and that feeds their imagination a bit more. But that is just what they imagine. If you must remember something of what happened today, please remember this: You are not what others think about you. Those are their thoughts, not you. You are not what you think you are, those are your thoughts, not you. Look deep inside yourself with your heart and feel what it has to tell you about yourself. Once you listen to your heart, you will discover the truly amazing human being that you are."

The moment of closing the door that leaves me alone with the chance to dress again has always made my heartbeat speed up. After I put on the bed the clothes I am about to dress, including corsets, shape enhancers, breast forms, wigs, and jewelry, and staring at it all, I start thinking about the "transformation" I am about to go through. As I start to get prepared and look at myself in the mirror from time to time at how my physical appearance is changing, my heart continues pounding strong and faster as if wanting to jump out of my chest. It is like something is becoming alive inside me and the thought that I am transforming myself changes. I am letting the woman in me come out and express herself. I understand now, for me, there is really no transformation going on. It is just the way to prepare the physical body to meet the soul. And when that happens, as soon as I have finished and achieved the female image I want, my heart slows down and I feel released, happy, and free. One day I will be out there in real life and not under locked doors on my own. Until then, it is wonderful to feel how my heart pounds knowing who I am.

Me Being Me

There were times when dressing and expressing my feminine self was an experience with mixed emotions. It was in my earlier times when I was still trying to understand my gender issues. It was wonderful when I was dressing, the whole process was a joy and I felt amazing every second of it for all the time it lasted. But it was completely the opposite when it was time to undress and get back to my usual boy look that I disliked so much. Switching back caused me sadness, depression, and confusion, and most of the time I was going to sleep immediately after that trying to forget those uncomfortable feelings. That situation happened many times and I knew it was related to feeling I was doing something wrong. It was like going from a wonderful state of joy down to a negative state of mind. Maybe it was like feeling guilty or some sort of hate towards my "male side". With time I learned that when I was dressing it was just me being me and there is no guilt on that. What I was told during childhood about "boys don't wear dresses and makeup" was conditioning my thoughts and feelings and that shouldn't be. It was somebody else's opinion, not mine. When I reached that understanding, I enjoyed my times "en-femme" far more because whenever I was "switching back" in my physical appearance I realized it was not the clothes and makeup that made me feel feminine. My feminine self exists beyond the external look I can achieve, is growing in awareness with time, and remains even if I change clothes because it's not just a part of me, it's me, it's who I am.

Feminine Side

"You have to be more in touch with your feminine side", I was told by a girlfriend when I was young. I had a bad temper, acting very impulsive and suppressing emotions to show I was strong and had no weaknesses. Those were the times of denial I went through about my gender identity when I was young, so it sounded uncomfortable to me when she said that. My behavior was an unconscious cover of what was happening inside me. I didn't know it then, but I know it now. I was trying hard to convince myself about being a young man and trying to ignore the voice of the girl inside me. My girlfriend didn't know about my gender identity issues but she was clever and had a very good perception. "There is nothing wrong with being sensitive, vulnerable and let your heart be touched by emotions and feelings and act freely from there. That applies equally to men and women. That is the only way you can openly and sincerely get to know the real you and let others know the real you too", she said. By getting in touch with my feminine side she was not talking about dressing as a girl, of course. It was not something for the outside. It was to connect deeply and honestly with the source of my personality and my essence to discover who I was. I didn't agree with her because of the way I was thinking at that time but the years that passed and all I learned and experienced later showed me she was right.

When I decided to get in touch with my feminine side, I discovered I was forcing my "male side" to hide my "female side" and was pushing her back. Becoming aware of this helped me to give up that useless internal fight. When the fight stopped, I was able to see the real me with my defects and virtues and accepted myself for the whole of who I am, a female soul in touch with a masculine side and not the other way around.

"Who is she?", my daughter asked when she was eight years old and was looking at the screen of my PC. I was sure I had locked the screen after leaving my desk, but my daughter had pressed the keyboard and the screen was activated again showing my latest activity. I had logged in to Facebook with my female profile after several months of being offline and had forgotten to log out, so my daughter was actually looking at my picture dressed as a girl and that was the first and only time something like that happened at home. "She is a friend", I answered nervous thinking she could recognize me behind all that makeup and the wig. I could have closed the screen but didn't want her to suspect there was something I didn't want her to see. "What is her name?", she asked while reading "Karen Lyra" just below the profile picture. "How do you know her?", she asked me. "Well, I know very little about her", I said, and it was true; I was still finding out "who I was" in terms of my gender identity and didn't know enough about my "inner girl". "But you said she is your friend, you should know. Unless she has not told you much about her...", "Yes, that's right. I have not seen her in a while so we haven't talked for some time", I replied remembering that I hadn't been dressing for a long while those days. My daughter continued: "Maybe she has secrets? A hidden identity, perhaps?", she said, and I was surprised at her questions. My daughter has always been very curious. She has a great imagination and can't stop asking questions all the time. "I think you are right, sweetheart", I said and closed the Facebook window to avoid more questions. "Maybe she hides her identity because she has superpowers, like a superhero!", my daughter said excited at her idea. "Well, I don't think she has superpowers, but I will ask her next time I meet her. Now let's go", I said closing the conversation. "She is pretty", my daughter said and immediately went out of the room leaving me alone and wondering about her words. I was relieved that she didn't recognize me in that picture and smiled at her "compliment", but more than anything, she left me wondering. I am keeping secrets and hidden identity, as my daughter said. And it doesn't feel good to do it that way. What could happen if one day my daughter or any of my relatives sees a picture of me as a female and can recognize me? Would it be better if I come out to them first before they end up finding out somehow? It is difficult to live like that, to know I am lying to my loved ones. I felt the need of taking that load from me.

Even though I was not into religion for a long time, I went to a Catholic church one day and looked for a priest. I told him I wanted to confess. He was very open and friendly. I said that I am married and have children, but I like dressing as a woman in secret as I have felt I wanted to be a girl since I was five years old. My voice was trembling when I said all that. It was the first time I spoke those words face-to-face with another person. I thought the priest was going to give me a long speech saying what I was doing was wrong, and that I should change my behavior because I was lying to my family and all that is a sin. The words of the priest were very different: "God loves and forgives, but first of all, you must look into your heart with love and deeply question yourself. That's the only way you will know if you are being true to yourself or if you are lying to yourself."

Several years ago, I read news about a local rock band that was popular when I was a teenager. They were about to perform live at a festival after a long time and were in the headlines because all the original members were the same, but their vocalist was now presenting as a woman. She had come out as transgender and transitioned going through hormones and surgery to live as the female she felt she was born to be. People were very curious about how her performance would be with the band and what the reaction of the fans was going to be. I was talking about that with some friends and one of them referred to the vocalist and said: "He can change his appearance, the way he behaves, he can change parts of his body, he can insist he is a woman and even may have an ID saying he is female. However, in the end, his sex chromosomes say the truth about what gender he is". For him, everything was about gender came down to the sex chromosomes we have. "XX for females and XY for males, that's it. No surgery can change that", he said. Another friend pointed out cases where anatomy and chromosomes don't obey the rule. There are always exceptions to the rule. I tried to explain to my friend about gender identity and the fact that most of the time it matches our anatomy but in many other cases it doesn't and that is what happens to transgender people. He didn't accept that, and the discussion went on for a while without reaching an agreement.

We all have different positions we take based on what we have learned, our beliefs, and the experiences we have lived. Changing our minds is always difficult especially if it challenges our core beliefs, but many times we have to do that to understand others better and grow as people.

"What would you do if I tell you I am transgender and want to transition and live as a woman like the vocalist of that band?", I asked my friend. He stared at me confused. "That's not going to happen. You are not transgender", he said. "Imagine if it does happen and I am. What would you do?", I insisted, and he remained silent for a while until he said: "Our friendship goes beyond our differences. If you were that vocalist, I would play the guitar to perform at your side too."

There was something I realized when I started wearing women's clothes as I began discovering my feelings about my gender identity. Every time I tried some lingerie, skirts, dresses, shoes, and makeup, I enjoyed it so much that I wanted more. After I tried red lipstick once, I wanted to try pink and then different colors and tones. The same happened with skirts and dresses. I wanted to see myself in different outfits, and different styles and I was amazed at how my attitude changed and maybe adapted to the look I was trying to achieve.

As a child and teenager, I was borrowing my sister's stuff and sometimes my mother's, but I was obviously restricted to their taste and size, and many times I was left without the chance for a new look. I remember discovering myself looking at fashion magazines my sister used to read and felt the strong desire to try a look of some of the female models I found there. Of course, that was difficult then and even later when I was able to buy that same dress, have a similar hairstyle and color (with the help of a wig), try the makeup that was going with that outfit, etc. I never had all the female stuff I wished I could have but I enjoyed what I had as much as I could until today.

Sometimes I felt discouraged at not being able to feel good about the results of my female appearance, but I kept on trying, learning, reading, practicing, watching video tutorials, and, more than anything, looking at women. Especially looking at women.

Months ago I watched the movie "The Danish Girl" on an airplane during a business trip and I remember how much I loved the scene when Lili, the main character, was looking at women and how they moved their hands and tilted their heads and she was trying to do the same. It was funny I found myself following her mannerisms at that same time while watching the movie.

I can wear the most wonderful dress, shoes, makeup, and hairstyle, but without the attitude, I can't feel good about the look I want to achieve. The outfit helps but doesn't make the woman.

There are brands of female apparel that are recognized immediately by the logos or colors they use. They could be brands of clothes, shoes, handbags, makeup, wigs, lingerie, etc. and their marketing campaign has been designed to capture the attention of potential buyers and get the loyalty of the already existing ones. There are some iconic brands that I relate with femininity more than any others but there is none like Victoria's Secret for me. I can't explain why but for me there is something magical with Victoria's Secret that keeps me in tune with my female identity.

When traveling, I always go to the duty-free at the airports and walk around to see what's new and, every time I walk around Victoria's Secret section, I cannot help it and let myself be hypnotized by the pink colors, the smell of the perfumes, the sexy look of the supermodels in lingerie on the posters on the walls, their amazing makeup, their gorgeous bodies, their sultry eyes, their confident look... How could I deny wanting to be one of them?

When I started travelling and taking my female clothes in my luggage, I felt nervous at customs thinking that maybe one day somebody could stop me for a routine check of my bag. At that time I was taking very few female clothes with me but as I was gaining more confidence and I was never stopped at customs, I felt comfortable taking more of my female clothes, shoes, makeup, wigs, etc. I was traveling with a very big bag and it was almost full of my female stuff with very few male clothing articles. How was I going to explain to an officer who all those clothes belonged to? How to explain there is a men's business suit mixed with platform high heels, wigs, lingerie, makeup, female jewelry all together? I wished I would never have to face that situation.

On one of my international business trips, I bought at the duty-free a large Victoria's Secret Bombshell makeup kit that I couldn't resist after looking at the sultry eyes of the supermodel Candice Swanepoel that was on the cover of the box. Her magical sexy eyes and partially opened lips make her whole facial expression hypnotic. How confident she looked is one of the things I love about her.

I put the makeup box inside my backpack thinking how much fun I was going to have with it at the hotel where I was going to stay. I took my luggage from the baggage claim belt and walked to the customs section to leave the airport. One officer asked me if I was carrying anything that I shouldn't in my luggage. I said I wasn't and he asked me to put my luggage and backpack on the belt to pass through the x-ray machine. I had done that so many times that I didn't feel nervous at all. The officer who was operating the machine was a lady. She was looking at the screen and stopped the belt once my luggage and backpack had passed through and then she ran it backwards to have a second look to my stuff. I saw her face and she seemed to have found something that caught her attention. She asked me if I was carrying belts and jackets in my bags.

101

I was carrying only one belt and no jacket at all and didn't know what she was talking about. She saw me doubting and then said she needed to check my bags. There were many people lined up behind me and my bags were going to be opened by the customs officer. I have seen that happen to other passengers before. All the content of their bags was taken out and fully exposed for inspection. I became nervous thinking on the dresses, lingerie, high heels, wigs, jewelry, makeup, corsets, etc. that I had in my luggage and were going to be taken out for an inspection. What were people going to say once they could see all that I was carrying with me? I imagined the possible scene and felt it could be very embarrassing. I thought I should have taken less of my female things in my bag, but I had gotten too excited when packing before travelling. The officer noticed I was not calm and said, "If you are not bringing with your luggage anything that you shouldn't, you don't need to be nervous". I was not bringing anything illegal, but I was going to be exposed and was nervous because I didn't want that to happen. There is a first time for everything, they say. I had never been stopped at customs before over many years of international travels. I tried to calm down and look completely normal as I had nothing illegal to hide..., but I had so much hidden about myself. She opened my backpack and took out a couple of books, my laptop, and the bag with the Victoria's Secret makeup kit that I had just bought in the duty free.

- You have some more of this in your other bag, right? – she asked. Being a woman and obviously experienced in x-ray images, she must had noticed some of the articles I was carrying that were unmistakably women's apparel and stuff. She was holding the makeup kit box inspecting if it was sealed. I looked at the confidence of Candice Swanepoel on the cover of the box. A very confident woman. How I wanted to have the confidence of such woman in that moment. How I wanted to have just a bit of it for me right there. I took a deep breath.

- Yes, I do. – I answered trying my best to sound confident and unconcerned. It felt good to change from my original nervous attitude.

- Do you resell those makeup articles? – she asked.

- No. I don't sell or resell. I work with makeup. – I answered spontaneously looking at Candice's eyes looking at me from the Victoria's Secret makeup box cover. I had just said to the customs officer that I worked with makeup and that would lead to more questions that could reveal more about my secret, but I was not feeling uneasy.

- Are you carrying jackets and belts on that big bag? – she insisted on her original question. I thought a bit on what she could have seen with the x-ray that made her wonder about the contents of my bag. Having clearer thoughts by feeling positive about how to deal with the situation, I found myself sure about what was causing her to ask me about jackets and belts.

- I am not carrying jackets but I am carrying two corsets. One is an under bust corset and the other one is a full corset with half cups. They are of the steel boned type with metal clasps at the front. Maybe that's what you have seen. – I answered naturally when she opened the zipper of my bag and noticed one of the corsets on top of everything I had there. The embarrassed scene

I was trying to avoid was about to begin but I was feeling assertive and decided to face it with confidence.

- I see. – she said, satisfied at finding out what I was saying was the truth. Then she gave a quick glance at the contents that were on top wrapped in plastic bags. There was another makeup box, she moved it a bit and the heels of my 6" black stilettos appeared. She looked at me with a puzzled smile, put the makeup box back in its place covering the stilettos and slightly touching on the top of some of the other colorful clothing articles to finally tell me she had finished and I could close my bags and leave.

- Thank you, officer. – I said. Why didn't she take out all the articles of my bag for a whole inspection as she should have done? I will never know but can imagine several reasons. I guess it had to do with how I changed my attitude. I know I need to work more on that to build my confidence. I closed my large bag feeling relieved and happy. I put my laptop and books into my backpack and then grabbed the Victoria's Secret makeup box. I looked at its cover before putting it back into my backpack and I said: "Thank you, Candice."

"What are they thinking? There must be something wrong with them. Why do they want to dress as someone of the opposite sex? It's not normal!". That was my dad one day a couple of years ago when we were at the doctor waiting for his medical appointment and he realized the woman at the cover of the magazine he picked from the table was a transgender model as it was briefly described there. She was Carmen Carrera. I had recognized her immediately even before reading her name below her photo.

My father didn't know at all who she was but was really upset. "Why did this magazine make that choice for their cover? This is so wrong!", he insisted. I kept myself in silence admiring the beautiful Carmen Carrera. It was a great photo in which she looked so confident and gorgeous. I know my father's position against transgender people and the LGBT community in general and although I am not planning to tell him I am transgender, I didn't want to let the opportunity pass without expressing my opinion. "I don't think there is something wrong with people like her. I think there is something wrong with us in the society when we are not open to understand that there are people that think and feel different from what we have been considering as standard and they are not hurting anybody by trying to be happy living their lives as they feel." I was speaking for me, but he didn't know. He was clearly not expecting that from me although he considers me as a very openminded person. "Son, you might be married and have children but you are confused as so many people of your generation is now, but I am not", he said and put the magazine back on the table as his name was called from the doctor's room. He got in and I waited out. I looked at the table again. There were several magazines and at least three of them had beautiful female models on their covers but my dad picked the one with Carmen Carrera. I know him well. He felt attracted to the gorgeous female he saw but he was not going to accept it because she was transgender. "Yes, dad. You are not confused as you say I am.", I thought and smiled.

"Why would someone decide to live as a person of the opposite gender?", was the opening question of a TV program in which the story of Angela Ponce, the Spanish model that was going to become the first transgender woman to participate in Miss Universe, was going to be covered. I am transgender but became aware of my gender identity late in life. I am not out in real life and can't transition now so I can only imagine what those wonderful human beings like Angela have gone through to achieve their dreams and live the life they have always known they should.

At home we watched part of the Miss Universe contest of that year with my family. Nobody at home was aware of the fact that Angela Ponce was a transgender woman, except me. It was interesting to hear their positive comments about her because they are not supportive to the LGBT community, but they didn't know her background until I told them her story. They were shocked and thought I was joking because that was something impossible for them. "But it is", I said.

I was thinking and trying to get into Angela's heart the moment she was modeling together with all those other beautiful women of the world. How much she had imagined that moment and finally her dream was a wonderful reality.

I remember her words when she was interviewed after she didn't make it to the final round of the contest. She was asked how she felt about not making it to the finals and she said: "I don't need to win Miss Universe. I only need to be here", and that phrase was so meaningful and inspiring to me and I believe to many other girls like us. They were words that summarize my dearest and deepest desire. I wish I could live as a woman because I want to be here being myself. That would be my answer to the original question of this post but there is something else. "Why would someone decide to live as a person of the opposite gender?", I don't see it as "the opposite gender". It's my real gender, have always been but, as for many girls like me, I was born with a different body and became aware of my gender identity maybe a little bit late in life. However, it is better late than never so I keep my hopes high that one day I will live the life I dream.

105

Finding people that inspired me to live my gender identity was also part of my personal search. As it happened with Angela Ponce and earlier with Jenna Talackova that meant a major breakthrough in the beauty contests for being not cisgender women but were let to participate, I didn't know if there was any company selling women clothes or women stuff in general that were supporting transgender women including them in their marketing campaigns. Maybe they were, but I couldn't find any.

I believe there was, and still is, a lot of prejudice that prevents many commercial companies to openly support transgender people, men or women, or anyone identifying themselves somewhere in the gender spectrum. Maybe they are afraid of taking that step and then find they get resistance from customers which may cause their sales to go down. At the end, to get more sales and make money is the main target of those companies, even though they may support other causes or social initiatives like women empowerment for example, but not including transgender women on those campaigns so far, at least from what I had seen.

Fashions shows were of my favorite programs to watch. Among them, the Victoria's Secret fashion shows were of those I wouldn't miss. I could spend hours watching and repeating them when I had that chance to watch them on YouTube. Supermodels have always amazed and inspired me since I was young and learning about the female image and attitude I felt more identified with. That's what I felt while looking at those women. Nothing sexual, nothing erotic. I just enjoyed seen supermodels enjoying themselves, having fun, being themselves while wearing different outfits. I loved that but have always been clear the outside beauty is evident, but to cultivate the inner beauty that we all have and is what matters the most to me.

As most aspects of whatever happens around us, the modeling world has also some problems that goes on in the background without us knowing. Fashion shows like Victoria's Secret were taken by some as a way of encouraging women to objectify themselves to impress men. The marketing chief of the company made statements about why the show was not incorporating transgender women and also plus-size models. He faced strong criticism for what he said and later he left the company. I believe we are getting more conscious in our society about the effect and impact some things have now in our society that we may have not considered before.

For me it was a delight to look the Victoria's Secret Angels catwalks, get submerged in those scenes and imagine what could have been if I could have had the chance to become a model and be part of that sort of magic world. I was always wondering if one day one of those supermodel angels was going to be a transwoman. The last official Victoria's Secret show was in December 2018 and then the show was cancelled, something I believe was in correlation with the criticism faced by the marketing chief of the company, and maybe a new strategy of the company to change its image to move forward in the industry. Maybe it was because of all those

106

events that in 2019 Victoria's Secret signed their first transwoman model, the beautiful Brazilian Valentina Sampaio. I loved so much to read this news and was so excited about it. Later I read Valentina's comment: "This represents a victory for society, not just the trans community but for all people who are currently underrepresented in fashion", and couldn't feel more than in agreement with her.

Valentina Sampaio became another inspiration to me and a signal of hope that, although there is still a long way to go, the world is really opening to accept diversity and let people be who they really are.

Before the time of the social networks as we know them now, there were several other ways to get in touch with people around the world with whom we could share interests. I remembered I built a website using the GeoCities platform that was free and with tools to build a webpage on my own without knowing much about it. I didn't post any picture because at that moment I didn't have a digital camera nor chances to dress fully and take pictures of myself. Building that page was mainly to share some of my experiences crossdressing and that was the first time I shared something like that about myself. But webpages were static and not interactive.

Later I found a site named URNA (U Are Not Alone) and immediately got caught by it. It was very interactive and that was what I was looking for, besides the chance of posting a public profile and getting comments, votes, etc. It was in URNA that I posted my first photo dressed completely as a woman and it felt very liberating. I was starting to have presence in the Internet as a female and couldn't felt any happier.

I chatted with girls like me, most of the times, but also with men who were openly saying they were straight but had interest in transgender girls. That was a bit confusing for me and couldn't understand them very well. None of my interactions in the chat rooms were of sexual nature, not even in private. With time I realized many people liked to fantasize having conversations of sexual nature, exchanging photos of them naked or very sexually explicit. I learned it was called Cyber Sex but I was not into it. During one of my purges I deleted my profile in URNA and lost all those pictures I took. I wish I could have had a backup of them, but all were lost.

When I restarted crossdressing while I was already married and had my gender therapy sessions, the therapist opened a private group in Facebook and so I had to open a profile there. Besides the private group of the gender sessions where I had some friends, I tried joining some other groups to meet more people, virtually. I value a lot what I learned from the people I got in touch with. There was a wonderful woman from Argentina that I met during the gender therapy sessions. We became good friends I guess because we both speak Spanish as our mother language and shared the Latin American culture origins and, we were married and had children. She became a reference for me. While she moved forward with transition and live full time as a woman, I stayed in the closet and I could see how wide she spread her wings and how far she flew wishing I could follow her path one day. She is living a happy life now, after several years of having difficult times. She is a brave and wonderful human being and I admire her. She always encouraged me to live according to my feelings and to be honest with myself. I have been honest with myself and finally accepted and embraced who I am, but I am still pending to live according to my feelings towards gender identity as she is doing.

I found several online stores on social networks where I could buy clothes and accessories to achieve the female image I wanted. I was following an online store named "Glamour Boutique"

108

on Facebook and I liked the items they were selling. I was about to make an appointment to visit their store for a makeover and buy onsite, but I was not traveling to the United States soon. I bought from them some wigs, shoes, lingerie, breast forms, corsets, gaffs, and body shape enhancers for hips and butt. I really loved all that I could buy from them and how they fit me. I continue buying from them from time to time and I am always satisfied.

A couple of years ago I found in Facebook that "Glamour Boutique" was promoting a sort of beauty contest for crossdressers and transgender people they named "Glamour Girl". I was very excited and thought that could be my chance to take part in a modeling event as a woman, a dream I had since I was a kid. It was a virtual contest so that made it easier for me. I looked for more information about it and I discovered there were already many girls submitting their pictures and they were amazingly gorgeous. The participants were voting for their favorites, and I couldn't believe how beautiful and feminine they looked. I was impressed and I wished I could look like them and although I was feeling satisfied with my feminine look, I knew there were many things I could do to get better results with my makeup and overall image to take good pictures. I took some pictures in a black mini dress with 6" high heels and fishnets, long dark chocolate brown hair and the best makeup I could, including false eyelashes and trimmed eyebrows that I learned how to make them look feminine when I dress in female clothes but still keeping them "neutral" so they are not much noticeable when I was in male clothes. I took several pictures with that look and posted them in my Facebook page, and I was surprised at how many people liked them and the beautiful comments I received. I felt encouraged and decided to submit my pictures to the beauty contest of Glamour Boutique and so I did. The day after I did that, I didn't feel good. One thing was to share my pictures in Facebook or Instagram in my private profiles where I was the only one giving access to the people I wanted to see what I was sharing. Of course, there was always the risk of having someone using my pictures somewhere else, but I didn't think much about it because there were so many beautiful and gorgeous girls out there that I would pass unnoticeable. By submitting my pictures to the contest, I was somehow making myself available openly in a public resource. I didn't feel good and felt worried, but it was done.

I kept on posting some pictures on Facebook and Instagram and I was getting more likes than I thought I could get and more friend requests than I had in my male profile. That was something that surprised me a lot. When I had some personal project that I wanted to promote through social media with my male profile, things never went smoothly and I had to work hard to attract visitors, potential customers, or just friends. But using my female profile things were happening without me doing anything special. Why? Once I had a funny thought: being "Karen" was giving me a sort of "superpower" that was making things work and flow naturally. So, I had a "hidden identity", like superheroes, and whenever I was in that role, things were going to work. The truth is that I was not very active on social networks as a female; I was only posting a picture every one or two weeks and I was offline for a couple of weeks every other time. My Facebook profile as a girl grew unexpectedly in the number of friends and it was also growing fast in followers on Instagram. The thought of being reached by someone I could know in real life scared me, so I closed and deleted those profiles. I felt better when I did that, at least for a while. Then I missed the people I was in touch with. I was not there for the likes and comments I could get but for the people I could make friends with, real friendships even if it was virtual. I preferred to

109

stay aside from the social networks for some time and after three or four months I came back. I hadn't even checked my email during that time. I was kind of resuming my dressing in female clothes after that "virtual purge" and wanted to start with a different look. I wanted to try being blonde which was more my natural hair color.

When I entered the website of Glamour Boutique to buy a blonde wig, I remembered the photo beauty contest and felt curious about the results. I was like three months late checking the results and was stunned at what I found. I had won first place in the "Cougars" category and was one of three girls that were winners in each category of the "Glamour Girl" contest of 2018. That was incredible! I couldn't believe that. I didn't want to be noticed but... there I was. When I checked my email, I found a message from Glamour Boutique saying that I had won a prize for getting first place in my category and I could choose some items they would send me for free. I got a new pair of breast forms and a new wig and felt so happy once I had them with me and was able to try them. I am still surprised and cannot believe how something like that could have happened.

That experience helped me to gain confidence about myself. I am a believer that confidence should come from ourselves, same as validation. What comes from the outside helps but can also generate a distorted impression, no matter we can take it as "right" or "wrong". However, one way or the other, I think we are looking to feel we belong, to feel validated, to feel we are liked and loved, and when this happens through the virtuality of the social networks it is also an important source of information to understand ourselves and question what we are projecting to others and how they are seeing us comparing to how we see ourselves.

There are people that inspire us and become like role models at some point of our life. We choose them because of what they mean to us and is something we value, love, admire, desire or because they are a source of inspiration to us that we can't explain well. It's just something we feel. They may have done something special and we relate to it, finding a particular meaning for us and we would take them as the example we want to follow. It may happen that we get impressed by the look or attitude of a person and without knowing anything about who they are, what they do or what they are going through, we feel attracted to them and can't explain why.

One very special friend of mine asked me who are the women that inspire me or I think about when I dress in female clothes. We all have different preferences and I believe it has to do with the image of that given person as a whole; what we see outside and what is projected from their inside together. But everyone perceives differently and sometimes we can't explain why we like a person. We just feel something special about that person and that's it. Maybe because I had gender identity issues from a very young age my main source of inspiration were women, as far as I remember, the ones that caused my feelings of being feminine growing up. I dreamed of becoming like them one day.

Caroline Cossey was my first and main one, and she continues to be. Her story was an inspiration for me when I was a teenager. I learned about other transsexuals, but she was the first for me, the source of undeniable inspiration that my dream could come true as she made hers come true.

After Caroline Cossey I was captivated by the supermodel Cindy Crawford. Her image was another undeniable inspiration for me and I was in love with her wishing I could be a model like her one day. I was dreaming too much, but dreams are like that, right? I remember watching her modeling and then trying to catwalk like her when I was wearing high heels.

A little time passed by and then something similar happened when I heard the voice of Shania Twain singing "You're still the one". I still have the collection of all her albums. It was not just her music. It was what I felt whenever I was watching her videos or listening to her music and wishing one day I could also be performing on a stage. I was dreaming again, I know, but loved to dream it that way. I had the chance to go to one of her concerts and see her live. She was the image of femininity I wanted for me.

Several years later, after I went through a long phase of denial about my gender identity and I was not dressing in female clothes anymore, I was watching TV and for the first time had the chance to watch one of those Victoria's Secret fashion shows. I was impressed by the event itself and of course by the look of the supermodels, the way they walked in high heels, looked, how they moved, blew kisses, winked, their lingerie, makeup, hair…, and all my thoughts about my wishes of being a woman came together to break my resistance at that time. All the models were gorgeous, sexy and so incredibly beautiful but it was the Brazilian Alessandra Ambrosio that caused my heart to stop. I couldn't stop looking at her and having a growing and unstoppable

111

desire that I had to dress again. Many times, when I dressed, I was trying to learn from her makeup and style. I am sure I may have achieved very little and I was dreaming again, but why not? I have followed her for many years.

During the last decade that I have been dressing female clothes more than ever in my life, I always have background music that uplifts me, that makes me feel feminine, that helps me bring my female self out. That was what happened in the past with Shania Twain when I was listening to her songs or watching her videos and it happened exactly the same with Taylor Swift for the last five years or so. I let her videos play one after another while I prepared myself to get dressed, finish my makeup, put on my lingerie, dresses, heels, wigs. I find inspiration in her music and many of her lyrics. That's why I use many short phrases of her lyrics on some of my posts in social networks for some time. Whenever I listen to her music it takes me immediately to the time when I tried the most to find myself and to discover who I am to finally become aware of my gender identity and accepted myself.

There are many more women that I have been following for years specially the ones that went through transition to live the lives they dreamed. I was following them for some time before their transition like Andreja Pejic, Carmen Carrera, Siobhan Atwell, Victoria Volkova, Kayla Autumn Ward, Carolina Gutierrez, and Valentina Sampaio. Following them, reading about them, listening to them whenever it was possible and watching how they became the human beings they dreamed was not only a wonderful source of inspiration for me but a light of hope.

112

Getting closer to my fifties, being married, having and raising children, working, having lived almost all my life feeling challenged by my gender identity and sexuality issues have had effects, consequences. There is an aftermath that maybe I still can't measure fully. But who can?

Am I still in love with my wife? Am I raising my children properly? Am I being honest with my family and friends or am I a liar or a hypocrite? Am I thinking too much on the pain I could cause others if I live what I consider my truth but not thinking enough on the pain and consequences for myself for not living my life at its fullest? Am I asking myself these questions only because I am transgender? No. It has nothing to do with that, I am sure. Those are common questions all of us have asked or are still asking ourselves as we move forward with life. For me, they have to do with being transgender. For others might have to do with something different. We all have challenges in our lives, things we want to accomplish, things we want to live, to have. That's life. So, has being transgender had an impact in my marriage, my family, my job? Of course there is an impact and I don't feel it is necessary to go deep into the details of each case but I can say, overall, the impact is it has broadened my awareness about life, how I treat myself and how I treat others. Realizing and embracing the fact of being transgender has let me bring out different sides of my essence as a person, sides with lights and shadows, as we all have, that I have understood as fundamental to set the baseline of who I am and focus my life on growing as a human being regardless of my gender identity and my sexuality and help others grow as well if there is anything, no matter how little, I can do in that regard.

One person sent me a message a while ago. He was following me on Tumblr and leaving some comments on my posts that maybe were not on the side of what I wanted to read. There are always some people that seem they can't express themselves with respect if they have to say something in opposition to what somebody else is saying or when they want to criticize. When that happens I try to "clean the noise and dust" of what I am receiving to find what is at the core of the message because it can always be something from where I can learn and grow. It is not always an easy thing to do, but I try my best. "You are living a lie", he said, and a large list of expressions full of adjectives used with anger and intending to hurt pointing out that I was never going to be a woman because that is impossible. I read his lines a couple of times and didn't answer him but wrote some lines for myself that later I shared as another post on social networks:

"Why are you living a lie?", the mind asked the heart. "Don't get confused, dear Mind. I am not living a lie. I am just working on living our truth", answered the heart. "What is our truth?", asked the mind. "Something I have tried to tell you for so long, dear Mind, but you always seem to be busy with your thoughts.", answered the heart with a sigh. "Those thoughts are so important, dear Heart. We wouldn't be here if it weren't for me and my thoughts", said the

113

mind proudly. "Yes, it's true, dear Mind. We wouldn't be here... and we would feel happy.", replied the heart and the mind didn't understand so it went back into its thoughts about what was that of "feeling" happy.

I am conscious of my reality and conscious about how far I am from getting to where I would like to be on the road of my life. But I am also conscious of my dreams. I can let my imagination fly so high that maybe it becomes difficult to live with both feet on the ground all the time. Life is made of dreams, the ones that are born in our hearts, the ones we work on making come true, the ones we see becoming our reality, the ones we leave aside for whatever reason after we decide to walk away from the road we believed was taking us to where we thought we could reach them.

When I was growing up my mother told me many times when she found how I was getting frustrated at some challenges and things I wanted to happen soon: "Maybe it's not your time. Sooner or later it would be but maybe it is not now, and you should accept it. However, do not stand still. Work on preparing yourself for that moment you are thinking of and you will be ready to recognize it once it arrives, because it will". Her words were not related to my feelings of being transgender, as I never had the courage to open that conversation to her, but those words she said can continue to easily apply at this stage of my life. She used to say: "Autumn has to pass and be followed by Winter before you can see the flowers blooming in Spring..."

If there is one thing I regret in my life it is not having had the courage to talk to my mother about my gender identity issues. I always thought she must have suspected what I was going through when I was a kid. It sounds impossible for me to think I was so lucky to not have her discovering something that could have given her a strong clue about my crossdressing habits as a child and during the time I lived with her. I imagined many times having that conversation with her and reached a point in which I was sure I had to talk to her about it. How many things she could have told me about my childhood that could have let me understand things better? One day I took the decision and visited her to talk about what I have been hiding all my life. It took a lot of courage to make that decision, but the time had arrived. When I got to her place, I found she was crying. She had just come back from the doctor and had been diagnosed with cancer. Everything happens for a reason. I have always thought there are no coincidences in our lives. I couldn't tell her anything about myself that day and very soon she became very sick. I decided I didn't want to add stress to her condition as she was going to worry about me and my family, so I didn't say anything about my gender identity issues. Few months later she passed away.

During our lives there are people that touch our heart and soul like no others. Those are the people with whom we end being like an open book even if we think we are not that open to them. They can see deep in our hearts, even things we believe nobody can see, things we believe nobody will ever discover from us unless we speak. They know, they discover, they can unveil

114

those things we keep for ourselves no matter if we say something about it or not. We can feel who these persons of our lives are and feel a need to talk to them about those things we keep for ourselves that are burning our heart. However, it happens that we deny those feelings because they might open doors to fears and uncertainties that we believe we won't be able to handle. We can imagine what could happen if we speak and open one of those doors, but the fact is, we will never know unless we try. If we do, chances are we can be surprised finding those persons that can read our heart and soul like nobody else are there on the path that follows after that door is opened, and they become the angels we need to move forward. Their hearts are open wide and are just waiting for us to take the first step. We should pay attention and not miss our chance.

Coming Out

Sooner or later some things we have left pending to do will remind us they need to be done. The things we have deeply thought we wanted to happen will occur if we have not given up on them and have kept a focus and taking actions, even if it was only to take baby steps forward. When that has happened to me, I felt like something has come full circle in my life and marks the beginning of another stage.

When I was attending gender therapy several years ago, I decided to come out as transgender to one of two persons I was sure were going to support me when the time to decide and follow my gender transition was right for me. I wrote a coming out letter to one of them as an exercise suggested by the therapist and I was planning to meet that person to come out to her. Later I knew she was living abroad and I didn't send the letter. I wanted to have a face-to-face meeting with her, but it was not going to be possible. I thought on talking to the other person I had chosen. He was an old friend, the psychologist with whom I had sessions when I was a teenager. I never exposed my gender identity issues to him although I suspected he knew. Well, I have always kept him in my mind as someone that can become supportive and from whom I can receive professional guidance too. I tried to get in contact with him but it was not possible. Many times, as years went by, I imagined having that coming out meeting with him and opening myself fully to let all my experiences and feelings be known by someone else that cares about me. I felt a need to meet him, sooner or later, to close that circle, to do what I didn't do when I was a teenager.

Recently I was able to find him on Facebook. I sent him a message asking for a chance to meet him to talk about some very personal things. Due to the Covid-19 pandemic he was only attending via video calls. I wanted to have the face-to-face meeting in person, not via a video call. It was very important for me to show myself I have the courage to not be behind a screen and let my voice be heard directly, let my face to be seen, and it was also important for me to see his reaction and hear his feedback directly. I wanted to have the experience that way. He accepted to let me visit him at his consulting room and we set the date. I was thrilled at the thought that finally I was going to do it. The scenario under which I could openly talk to my friend about all I have been hidden for all my life was ready.

On the day that we were going to meet I was feeling nervous and anxious. So many questions were storming in my mind, so many emotions. Finally, I was there sitting in front of him. It was not possible for me to present myself as a woman, so I went dressed as male as I do in my day to day life at home with my family. We caught up on what happened in our lives after a long time of not seeing each other except for a couple of short casual encounters on the street years ago that didn't allow us to talk much. I had prepared my coming out speech to him, somehow. I had thought a lot on how to start opening myself to him. However, my mind went

116

blank after we finished updating each other about ourselves and then he asked me what was so important that I wanted to talk to him in person and in private. The moment had arrived.

- All my life I have identified myself with women, as one of them, wishing to be like them, to become one of them. I have had this feeling during all the stages of my life and felt confused and afraid wondering if something was wrong with me. You should remember we talked about how difficult it was for me to have a romantic relationship with girls when I was a teenager. The truth is that I liked them in a way that I wanted to be a girl. I started wearing my sister's and mother's dresses, shoes, lingerie and makeup when I was five years old. I did that always in secret and hiding from everyone. For some reason I had the idea that what I was doing shouldn't be known by others because it was something bad, something wrong. I didn't do that to get sexual pleasure from it. I did it because I wanted to see myself as a girl because I wanted to be a girl. I took many risks in my attempts to dress as a girl at home. However, I was never caught and I never talked to anybody about all this. I thought those feelings would eventually disappear as I was growing up, going to the university, have girlfriends, get married, have children. I was wrong. The gender identity issues didn't disappear. No matter how much I suppressed my compelling desires of crossdressing I found myself looking for ways to continue doing it... and it has been part of my life and continues today. I have reached an understanding that my real gender identity is female and that is why I cannot suppress it or get rid of it. It is who I am although I was not able to live my life accordingly given my family and job situation. I love my wife and children, but if I were not married and didn't have a family, I would have moved forward to change my life long ago and express myself as female living like the woman I feel I am openly to the world. For the last ten years I have been developing and increasing my crossdressing habits more and more, taking it very seriously, feeling I finally can be my true self whenever I can see the image of myself as female. I usually do that during business trips at rented apartments or hotel rooms and only by myself. Except for a couple of cases in which I have gone out as female at night alone, which exposed me to a dangerous and unpleasant sexual experience with a man too, I haven't shared the experience of being female with anybody in real life. When I am dressed as a woman, I feel I am expressing myself as I should because that is what I am: a woman that happens to have been born in a male body. I was looking for help and some years ago I had therapy with a gender therapist. The sessions were on video conference calls and not in person. After we talked the therapist said I have gender dysphoria and I am transgender. That was a reaffirmation for me and I felt happy to get her diagnosis. I felt like finally I knew what was happening to me. She suggested I should move forward with gender transition and start taking hormones. She wrote me a letter with the diagnosis of gender dysphoria and her recommendation to begin hormone replacement therapy with an endocrinologist. It was something I wanted but I was afraid because I haven't had experiences as a woman in real life plus the fact that I was not out to anybody in my family or friends yet. She said I didn't need to rush with my gender transition but needed to be conscious of my new awareness as female to work on that as that would be the only way to overcome gender dysphoria and finally feel at peace with myself to develop the life I want. She asked me about my sexual orientation too. Until that moment I didn't consider seriously that I liked men

117

and questioned myself. It was difficult because I couldn't say I liked or disliked men. However, with time, the more I dressed as a woman the more I also started to think that I wanted to be sexually with men. I don't see me as a man with another man, but I see myself as a woman with a man. That was not happening before but now it does and the feeling is increasing. All this has taken me to a point in which I can't take more time trying to hide my feelings, but I also can't come out to my family without a plan on how to continue with life and what to do after that. Letting them know all about me would mean breaking the family and I still have kids that depend on me. I love them. I don't want that. Not saying anything to my wife and children makes me feel guilty as I know I am lying to them and feel very bad about it. That's why I wanted to talk to you. I needed someone to whom I can say all this face to face and thought this person should be you. Right now, I feel liberated after having told you all this, getting it all out. It feels like taking a heavy load off of me, although the confusion about what I should I do remains.

I said all that making pauses to look at his reaction, the way he was looking at me in silence paying attention to everything I was saying, to my emotions, my expressions, my body language. When I finished, I felt surprised at how easily the words came out of me and how my thoughts were exposed without feeling embarrassed. It was a great feeling or realization. He didn't interrupt me or say a word and let my words flow out of me to let me say all I wanted. When I stopped speaking, I smiled at him saying that was all I had to say. He smiled back.

- Thank you for sharing all this with me. Do not worry, Eric. I have known you and your family for more than thirty years by now and have understood many of the things you all went through, beginning with your mother of course, and your sister too. The violence of your father, the divorce of your parents, the economic struggles, etc. All that helps me a lot to be able to assist and guide you because I have a background that is very valuable to assess your case. – he said in a comforting manner and not showing himself surprised at my confessions as if he really knew what I wanted to talk about.

After that we talked a lot about transgender people, the gender identity theories and what is going on in society that today is more open to accept different gender expressions although there is a long way to go to reach the level of acceptance needed so transgender people can express themselves freely and openly without the risk of suffering violence.

He told me about some cases of men that had therapy with him that had the same feelings I have. Some of them moved forward with gender transition and changed their identities to live as the women they felt they were. However, several of them didn't find happiness after they did that.

- There are many things we do as human beings that are a response to something that challenges us or makes us feel uncomfortable. It happens especially under scenarios of high pressure, fear or violence; we want to run away from those situations because they cause us heavy stress. When we feel that way we look for something that can make us feel protected from the pressure or violence and might end believing what we are doing defines who we are. We

118

don't acknowledge that it could be a coping mechanism, an escape of the reality that hurts us, the reality that we feel not capable to change or are too afraid to fight. We let anxiety drive our lives and unconsciously develop addictions that become the perfect coping mechanism to give us the balance we are looking for. So, sometimes, moving forward with gender transition in the case of people that believe they are transgender is like treating the symptom without knowing what is the root cause that generates that symptom. That is why it is so important to be very careful as it is very easy to believe gender transition is the answer to the question when in fact the problem is the wrong question has been asked. – he said and it sounded very reasonable and logical, but I didn't feel like what he was saying was my case. I understood that some of the cases of the persons he mentioned that moved through gender transition to live as women ended with a very unhappy and deeply depressed life because they were not really transgender. Their "coping mechanism", as he mentioned, had developed so strong and for such a long time that those persons felt it was their reality when it was proved by their own experiences it was not.

- But, how can we know when it is a coping mechanism and not something that we truly identify with, something we like and just feel comfortable doing it without harming anybody and enjoying seriously as that could give us the joy, satisfaction and inner peace of a personal realization experience? I am thinking on many of the transgender women that I have followed since I was a teenager. My role model, for example, is Caroline Cossey. She was a model in a James Bond movie of the 80's it was later found that she was transgender. I don't feel like she or others like her developed a crossdressing habit when they were children as a coping mechanism to overcome anxiety and end up following gender transition to live as women later. It couldn't just be because it was a coping mechanism they developed at a very young age. I believe there must have been something different, something else. Maybe after they accomplished gender transition they had other life challenges and problems like any of us and may not be fully happy today, but they do feel comfortable and in peace with their inner gender identity. How do I know if this is or this is not my case?

- Some of them are transgender, but you are not, Eric. In your case, knowing how dedicated to the details you are, how you obsessively study and research about what you want to understand, you have perfected your crossdressing practice year after year, improving it in such a way that to look as female as possible as you can has become an obsession for you. In your mind that means to do whatever is needed to create the perfect moment to build the perfect female image that you think you can achieve. That also involves thinking to be with men sexually as it is, for you, the natural unconscious following step that you should take once the image of you as a woman is already complete. You didn't think about being sexually with men before, but you do now because you need something more. This is the way it happens to an addict regardless of the matter of the addiction. You could have tried to find shelter in alcohol, drugs, sex, food, sports, study, music, and so many other practices that we know can be addictions, but we don't always call them that because it sounds bad. We all have addictions. Those are not just things that we like a bit from time to time and we can leave them without feeling compelled to go back to them. Addictions are those things that we like so much that we can't stop doing them. That is

119

exactly what happens to you with crossdressing. That is exactly what happens to some people with sports or food, for example. You were also a person that was very much into sports, some dangerous life risking extreme ones. You should have asked yourself why you were like that. What was behind all that? What were you trying to cope with? The practice of extreme sports gave you satisfaction but whenever you stopped them for some involuntary reason, you felt depressed and very unhappy. Right? That is what happens to an addict too when he or she can't fulfill their addiction needs. At the end, if you were committed so many times to stop crossdressing and you couldn't, you should have asked yourself the question of why you do it looking for what could have generated that strong need in you. For alcohol addicts the problem is not drinking alcohol. For drug addicts the problem is not taking drugs. The problem is what is causing them to drink alcohol or taking drugs. Your problem is what causes you to cross-dress, not the crossdressing action itself. Once you get to the root cause you will really understand what happens to you and that will give you the clarity you need to see things from a different perspective and challenge what you have believed about yourself so far so you can truly find who you are and what is going on with you. What do you think? Does it make sense? – he ended with a question willing to know my opinion as I was nodding while listening his words and statements.

All he said made perfect sense to me. It sounded logical and valid. I know he is a good and recognized professional and he also cares about me. That is why I took his words with respect and paid attention to all he said even though I don't think or believe that what he said applies exactly to my case. There are components to the analysis that he made of my case that don't match for me, but he challenged my beliefs with his statements and that is something I consider important and key thing to do in order to broaden my perspective and grow as a human being to expand my mind.

The weekend that followed our first meeting was one in which I thought and wrote a lot about what happened during our conversation because I heard so many things from him that I disagreed with. It was a challenging and not a very comfortable thing to do but I knew it was going to help me understand and be prepared for our next session.

A week later we met again. I asked him many questions and we went deeper into how my childhood was as there is exactly where my crossdressing started.

We talked about what I can remember of my home with my parents together when I was a child. I don't have memories of my parents fighting. They must have had their discussions but maybe they found a way to hide them from my sister and me. As my psychologist friend said, the fact that I don't remember the fights of my parents doesn't mean they didn't happen and affect me. He knew about that because of what he talked with my mother when she was having therapy with him. She must have told him many things I didn't know and will never know now that she died. I remember I was mostly a happy kid except for the moments when my father hit me or punished me very hard because I didn't want to eat a given food or I cried when falling down, or when I did something I was asked by him not to do or touch. Could it have been that maybe I don't remember but I openly and innocently expressed that I liked dresses, or he found I liked

120

girl's clothes and that made him mad so he treated me that way? I will never now but definitively a lot more happened at home before my parents got divorced and my father left us than the things I can remember.

Then we talked about how I went through phases of feeling comfortable crossdressing and then feeling guilty and stopping it completely for a while to end resuming my habit later and repeating the cycle all my life. After we talked a lot about that, and I shared critical experiences of my life, he said my crossdressing started when I was a kid to fight anxiety. For him, I developed crossdressing as a coping mechanism at an early age to search for a way to avoid the pressure and the violence of my father towards me by recognizing there was no violence against my sister or other girls that I knew. For him, in my mind, a strong belief was born: if girls are not hit then I wanted to be a girl. It was not a spontaneous thought at that young age. It was an instinctive answer to the situation I was living. It was conditioned by the circumstances. I disagreed with his statement although his reasoning was logical. He insisted that my case is the matter of an addiction to a coping mechanism to fight anxiety that I am also using to build a belief of my identity to justify my behavior. The root cause of what took me to express a female identity was not known by me as I was too young and didn't get any guidance because I never spoke up, so it was never addressed and not acknowledged.

- Eric, you, like many others I have known, don't need to come out of the closet as transgender because there is simply no closet to come out from as you are not transgender. Your crossdressing is only a coping mechanism you have let grow for so long to fight anxiety through your life with more or less intensity depending on the level of stress you were suffering in the different stages of your life. You could have switched to another coping mechanism, but because you found shelter in crossdressing since you were so young and it worked for you making you feel good, you always go back to it. You are not transgender, my friend. Because of that, it would be a mistake to try gender transition. We need to work on the root cause, not the symptom. - he concluded looking at me with a smile as if he was a teacher that had given me the answer to the most difficult question of an exam I was taking as his student.

It's been said that when we are told something we listen to what we want and don't listen to what we don't want. I try hard not to fall for that and keep myself open to listen things that I may not have considered because I don't like or maybe they just never came to my mind. I consider it is necessary to be open as there are so many things I don't know that I have to learn to have the best possible perspective about myself and reach an understanding of who I am and what my beliefs are.

If I compare what my friend the psychologist said with what the gender therapist that treated me years ago said, the latter told me I am transgender and I should transition. Now I hear the opposite from my friend the psychologist. At the end this it is not what I am told by some or not told by others, but I value what I hear from people who care about me and that includes things I may not agree with. At the end, the answer is in my heart and I know there is so much I

121

haven't experienced yet as the woman I feel I am to enlarge the source of my thoughts and feelings. There is a long way to go and a lot of things to experience, learn and understand.

Finding myself is a challenging quest and I have been dealing with it for all my life from the darkness and on my own, hiding from others what I believe is my true self. There is something that I need to do to change and move forward. Recently, a very close friend that I still don't know in person but with whom I have shared a lot and I love and respect, wrote me a message: "Karen, it is time to go out in public to find new insights about yourself". I agree with her and I am sure that is the mandatory next step for me. The quest is far from being finished. It's time to open the door that keeps me frozen under the clouds and walk through it to move out and finally experience my true self under the warm bright rays of a shining sun. We all deserve that.

Thank You

I take every opportunity of meeting people as a chance to learn and a way to see things from a different perspective of the one I usually have. I try to learn when I feel I am loved as well as when I feel I am not. For what matters is what has taken me to write all what I have shared in this book, I have felt loved by people that I am not lucky to meet in person but with whom I feel privileged to have built an open and honest relationship. To finish this book, I want to express my gratitude to all of them for their love, encouragement and support. Thanks to all of you, wherever you are, you have a place in my heart.

Printed in Great Britain
by Amazon